BUSINESS ISSUES, COMPETITION AND ENTREPRENEURSHIP

WHISTLEBLOWERS

SELECTED ISSUES AND PROTECTIONS

BUSINESS ISSUES, COMPETITION AND ENTREPRENEURSHIP

Additional books in this series can be found on Nova's website under the Series tab.

Additional e-books in this series can be found on Nova's website under the e-book tab.

BUSINESS ISSUES, COMPETITION AND ENTREPRENEURSHIP

WHISTLEBLOWERS

SELECTED ISSUES AND PROTECTIONS

ANDRE POPE
EDITOR

New York

LIBRARY OF CONGRESS CATALOGING-IN-PUBLICATION DATA

ISBN: 978-1-63482-290-9

Published by Nova Science Publishers, Inc. † New York

CONTENTS

PREFACE

Generally speaking, whistleblowers are those who expose misconduct (e.g., fraud, abuse, or illegal activity) within an organization. Legal protections for employees who report illegal misconduct by their employers have increased dramatically since the late 1970s when such protections were first adopted for federal employees in the Civil Service Reform Act of 1978. Since that time, with the enactment of the Whistleblower Protection Act of 1989, Congress has expanded such protections for federal employees. Congress has also established whistleblower protections for individuals in certain private-sector employment through the adoption of whistleblower provisions in at least 18 federal statutes. This book provides an overview of key aspects of the 18 selected federal statutes applicable to individuals in certain private-sector industries. It also examines steps OSHA has taken to include auto industry employees in its whistleblower program and the extent to which OSHA collaborated with DOT components to address potential safety violations; and the number of transportation-related whistleblower claims in the last 6 years and stakeholder-identified factors that may affect those numbers.

Chapter 1 – Intelligence whistleblowers are generally Intelligence Community (IC) employees or contractors who bring to light allegations of agency wrongdoings by, for example, disclosing information on such wrongdoings to congressional intelligence committees. Such disclosures can aid oversight of, or help curb misconduct within, intelligence agencies. However, intelligence whistleblowers could face retaliation from their employers for their disclosures, and the fear of such retaliation may deter whistleblowing. Congress and President Obama have taken measures to protect certain intelligence whistleblowers from retaliation, and thereby seemingly encourage these whistleblowers to disclose information on agency wrongdoing. These measures are the Intelligence Community Whistleblower Protection Act of 1998 (ICWPA), Presidential Policy Directive 19 (PPD-19), and Title VI of the Intelligence Authorization Act of 2014 (Title VI). Each of these measures details what disclosures fall within the scope of its protections, which generally include certain disclosures through government channels (e.g., disclosures to agency inspectors general or congressional intelligence committees). None of these measures protect against retaliation or potential criminal liability arising from disclosures to media sources. The ICWPA applies to both IC employees and contractors, whereas PPD-19 and Title VI appear to apply only to IC employees.

The ICWPA is the oldest of the three intelligence whistleblower protections and, of the three, provides the least amount of protection to those falling within its scope. The ICWPA does not explicitly prohibit retaliation against IC whistleblowers. Rather, it outlines procedures through which whistleblowers can disclose to the congressional intelligence committees information on "urgent concerns," such as violations of law or false statements to Congress. The ICWPA further contains no explicit mechanism for obtaining a remedy for retaliation stemming from disclosure of an urgent concern to Congress. It merely allows an IC whistleblower who has faced an adverse personnel action because he disclosed an urgent concern to the congressional intelligence committees to then use the ICWPA's disclosure procedures to inform the committees of the retaliation.

PPD-19, unlike the ICWPA, expressly prohibits an IC employee from taking an adverse personnel action or security clearance determination against another employee because of a protected disclosure. It additionally requires intelligence agencies to develop procedures for internally investigating, through agency Inspectors General, allegations of impermissible retaliation. After finding that impermissible retaliation has occurred, Inspectors General can recommend that agency heads take corrective action. When an employee has exhausted the internal review procedures that must be established under PPD-19, he can appeal to the Director of National Intelligence, who then has the discretion to convene a review panel. If it finds that improper retaliation occurred, the review panel can recommend that the agency head take remedial action.

Title VI seemingly codifies, and expands upon, some of the protections of PPD-19. Its protections, and modes of enforcement, differ depending on the type of retaliation alleged. More specifically, Title VI's protected disclosures and enforcement methods in the context of allegations of adverse personnel action are distinct from its protected disclosures and enforcement methods for allegations of adverse security clearance or information access determinations.

Chapter 2 – Legal protections for employees who report illegal misconduct by their employers have increased dramatically since the late 1970s when such protections were first adopted for federal employees in the Civil Service Reform Act of 1978. Since that time, with the enactment of the Whistleblower Protection Act of 1989, Congress has expanded such protections for federal employees. Congress has also established whistleblower protections for individuals in certain private-sector employment through the adoption of whistleblower provisions in at least 18 federal statutes. Among these statutes is the Sarbanes-Oxley Act, the FDA Food Safety Modernization Act, and the Dodd-Frank Wall Street Reform and Consumer Protection Act (Dodd-Frank Act).

In general, claims for relief under the 18 federal statutes follow a similar pattern. Complaints are typically filed with the Secretary of Labor, and an investigation is conducted. Following the investigation, an order is issued by the Secretary, and a party aggrieved by the order is generally permitted to appeal the Secretary's order to a federal court. However, because 18 different statutes are involved in prescribing whistleblower protections, some notable differences exist. For example, under the Department of Defense Authorization Act of 1987, individuals employed by defense contractors who engage in whistleblowing activities file complaints with the Inspector General rather than the Secretary of Labor. Under some of the statutes, including the Commercial Motor Vehicle Safety Act and the Dodd-Frank Act, the Secretary's preliminary order will become a final order if no objections are filed within a prescribed time period.

This report provides an overview of key aspects of the 18 selected federal statutes applicable to individuals in certain private-sector industries. It focuses on the protections provided to employees who believe they have been subject to retaliation, rather than on how or where alleged misconduct should be disclosed. In addition, the report also includes an overview of the Whistleblower Protection Act. While state law may also provide whistleblower protections for employees, this report focuses only on the aforementioned federal statutory provisions.

Chapter 3 – Transportation workers who "blow the whistle" on prohibited practices can help ensure that their employers comply with federal laws. Within the Department of Labor, OSHA investigates whistleblower claims, filed by transportation employees who believe their employers have retaliated against them for reporting unlawful practices. The Moving Ahead for Progress in the 21st Century Act (MAP-21), required OSHA to establish protections for auto industry employees and required GAO to review OSHA's efforts and transportation-related whistleblower claims. GAO examined (1) steps OSHA has taken to include auto industry employees in its whistleblower program and the extent to which OSHA collaborated with DOT components to address potential safety violations, and (2) the number of transportation-related whistleblower claims in the last 6 years and stakeholder-identified factors that may affect those numbers. GAO compared agency documents against key practices for collaboration, and interviewed federal agency officials and stakeholders representing transportation modes covered by these statutes to identify factors that may affect the number of whistleblower claims reported by OSHA.

In: Whistleblowers:
Editor: Andre Pope

ISBN: 978-1-63482-290-9

Chapter 1

INTELLIGENCE WHISTLEBLOWER PROTECTIONS: IN BRIEF*

Rodney M. Perry

SUMMARY

Intelligence whistleblowers are generally Intelligence Community (IC) employees or contractors who bring to light allegations of agency wrongdoings by, for example, disclosing information on such wrongdoings to congressional intelligence committees. Such disclosures can aid oversight of, or help curb misconduct within, intelligence agencies. However, intelligence whistleblowers could face retaliation from their employers for their disclosures, and the fear of such retaliation may deter whistleblowing. Congress and President Obama have taken measures to protect certain intelligence whistleblowers from retaliation, and thereby seemingly encourage these whistleblowers to disclose information on agency wrongdoing. These measures are the Intelligence Community Whistleblower Protection Act of 1998 (ICWPA), Presidential Policy Directive 19 (PPD-19), and Title VI of the Intelligence Authorization Act of 2014 (Title VI). Each of these measures details what disclosures fall within the scope of its protections, which generally include certain disclosures through government channels (e.g., disclosures to agency inspectors general or congressional intelligence

* This is an edited, reformatted and augmented version of a Congressional Research Service publication R43765, prepared for Members and Committees of Congress, dated October 23, 2014.

committees). None of these measures protect against retaliation or potential criminal liability arising from disclosures to media sources. The ICWPA applies to both IC employees and contractors, whereas PPD-19 and Title VI appear to apply only to IC employees.

The ICWPA is the oldest of the three intelligence whistleblower protections and, of the three, provides the least amount of protection to those falling within its scope. The ICWPA does not explicitly prohibit retaliation against IC whistleblowers. Rather, it outlines procedures through which whistleblowers can disclose to the congressional intelligence committees information on "urgent concerns," such as violations of law or false statements to Congress. The ICWPA further contains no explicit mechanism for obtaining a remedy for retaliation stemming from disclosure of an urgent concern to Congress. It merely allows an IC whistleblower who has faced an adverse personnel action because he disclosed an urgent concern to the congressional intelligence committees to then use the ICWPA's disclosure procedures to inform the committees of the retaliation.

PPD-19, unlike the ICWPA, expressly prohibits an IC employee from taking an adverse personnel action or security clearance determination against another employee because of a protected disclosure. It additionally requires intelligence agencies to develop procedures for internally investigating, through agency Inspectors General, allegations of impermissible retaliation. After finding that impermissible retaliation has occurred, Inspectors General can recommend that agency heads take corrective action. When an employee has exhausted the internal review procedures that must be established under PPD-19, he can appeal to the Director of National Intelligence, who then has the discretion to convene a review panel. If it finds that improper retaliation occurred, the review panel can recommend that the agency head take remedial action.

Title VI seemingly codifies, and expands upon, some of the protections of PPD-19. Its protections, and modes of enforcement, differ depending on the type of retaliation alleged. More specifically, Title VI's protected disclosures and enforcement methods in the context of allegations of adverse personnel action are distinct from its protected disclosures and enforcement methods for allegations of adverse security clearance or information access determinations.

INTRODUCTION

Generally speaking, whistleblowers are those who expose misconduct (e.g., fraud, abuse, or illegal activity) within an organization. In the context of the Intelligence Community (IC), whistleblowers are generally employees or contractors of federal intelligence agencies who bring to light information on agency wrongdoings. Whistleblowers disclose this information through government channels (e.g., the congressional intelligence committees or agency inspectors general) or to the media. Such disclosures can aid oversight of, and thereby curb misconduct within, intelligence agencies. When an IC whistleblower discloses information on alleged agency wrongdoing, he could face retaliation from his employer by, for example, being fired, demoted, or having his security clearance revoked.

The threat of retaliation may deter potential whistleblowers from disclosing information on agency wrongdoing. There is seemingly tension between the desire to eliminate this deterrence, and thus encourage whistleblowers to bring agency misconduct to light, and the need to protect government secrets which, if disclosed publicly, could be harmful to the country's national security interests. Apparently seeking to strike balance within this tension, Congress and President Obama have taken action to limit retaliation against IC whistleblowers for certain types of protected disclosures, which do not include disclosures to media sources. That is, IC whistleblowers who disclose information to media sources generally are unprotected against potential retaliation or criminal sanction.

There are three sources of protections against retaliation for IC whistleblowers: the Intelligence Community Whistleblower Protection Act of 1998 (ICWPA),[1] Presidential Policy Directive 19 (PPD-19),[2] and Title VI of the Intelligence Authorization Act for Fiscal Year 2014 (Title VI).[3] Before passing the ICWPA, which is the oldest of the three protections, Congress observed that intelligence whistleblowers apparently lacked protection against retaliation stemming from their disclosures of agency wrongdoings.[4] Whistleblower protections for federal employees are largely governed by the Whistleblower Protection Act (WPA), which Congress initially passed in 1989, and its amendments.[5] The WPA expressly excluded intelligence agency employees from its applicability, and thus initially left intelligence whistleblowers unprotected against retaliation.[6] The ICWPA seemingly represented Congress's attempt at filling this gap by extending protections to intelligence whistleblowers.

Though the ICWPA extended some protections to intelligence whistleblowers, it afforded such whistleblowers less protection than the WPA affords non-intelligence whistleblowers. However, protections for intelligence whistleblowers have strengthened over time. PPD-19, which President Obama issued in 2012, expanded upon the ICWPA's protections for some IC whistleblowers, and Title VI generally codified, and in some instances built upon, the protections of PPD-19. This report describes these three sources of IC whistleblower protection.

INTELLIGENCE COMMUNITY WHISTLEBLOWER PROTECTION ACT OF 1998

The ICWPA is the oldest of the three intelligence whistleblower protections. In passing the ICWPA, Congress observed that the threat of adverse personnel action to IC employees deterred them from whistleblowing.[7] This deterrence from whistleblowing, Congress found, may have been constricting the flow of information to congressional intelligence committees that the committees needed to properly perform their oversight responsibilities.[8] The ICWPA therefore permits IC employees and contractors to bring a complaint or disclose specified information to Congress, and outlines the procedures for doing so. However, the ICWPA does not expressly prohibit retaliation against IC whistleblowers for permissibly bringing a complaint or information to Congress and contains no explicit mechanism for obtaining a remedy for this retaliation. Rather, the ICWPA merely allows an IC whistleblower who has faced such retaliation to then use the act's disclosure procedures to inform the intelligence committees that the retaliation has occurred.

The ICWPA applies to employees of the Central Intelligence Agency, Defense Intelligence Agency, National Imagery and Mapping Agency, National Reconnaissance Office, National Security Agency, Federal Bureau of Investigation, and any other agency that the President determines has the principal function of conducting foreign intelligence or counterintelligence activities.[9] The ICWPA also applies to the employees of a contractor of any of the aforementioned agencies.[10] An employee seeking to bring a complaint or disclose information to Congress under the ICWPA is subject to two limitations: (1) the complaint or information must be related to an "urgent concern" as defined in the act; and (2) the employee must first bring the complaint or disclose the information to the agency head through the proper agency channels.

Under the ICWPA, IC employees and contractors can disclose to Congress only complaints and information that are "with respect to an urgent concern."[11] Under the act, an "urgent concern" can be one of three things.[12] First, it can be a "serious or flagrant" abuse, problem, violation of executive order or law, or deficiency in funding, agency administration, or agency operations involving classified information.[13] Second, an urgent concern can be a false statement to, or willful withholding from, Congress on an issue of material fact relating to intelligence activity funding, administration, or operation.[14] Third, an urgent concern can include adverse personnel action stemming from disclosure under the ICWPA.[15] A complaint or information that is not regarding one of these three "urgent concerns" is not covered by the ICWPA.[16]

IC employees and contractors must first bring complaints or information regarding "urgent concerns" to the agency head through proper agency channels, as described in the ICWPA, before bringing them to Congress. This generally requires first bringing a complaint or information to the agency's Inspector General or the Inspector General of the IC (IGIC),[17] who then has 14 calendar days to evaluate the credibility of the complaint or information.[18] Upon finding the complaint or information credible, the Inspector General must send notice of its finding, along with the complaint or information, to the agency head within the 14-calendar-day period for evaluation.[19] The agency head then has 7 calendar days from receipt of the Inspector General's notice to forward the notice, along with any of the agency head's comments, to the congressional intelligence committees.[20]

The ICWPA allows employees to contact intelligence committees directly if the Inspector General either does not find the complaint or information credible, or sends the agency head an inaccurate complaint or inaccurate information.[21] However, this ability to contact the intelligence committees directly is subject to two limitations. First, before making such contact, an employee or contractor must give the agency head a statement of the complaint or information through the Inspector General, along with notice of intent to contact the intelligence committees directly.[22] Second, the employee or contractor must follow the agency head's direction, given through the Inspector General, on compliance with appropriate security practices when contacting the intelligence committees.[23]

The ICWPA seemingly represents an attempt by Congress to fill a gap in federal whistleblower protections by extending such protections to IC whistleblowers where they were expressly excluded from the WPA and its amendments, which generally provide whistleblower protections to federal employees.[24] However, the ICWPA appears to afford IC whistleblowers fewer protections than the WPA affords non-intelligence whistleblowers. The WPA provides an employee with an individual right of action for prohibited retaliation, through which he can bring a claim against this agency in the Merit

Systems Protection Board (MSPB).[25] The MSPB can then provide several remedies, including, but not limited to, returning the individual to the position he would have been in if retaliation had not occurred, awarding back pay, and awarding any reasonable and foreseeable consequential damages.[26] If an employee's claim is unsuccessful before the MSPB, the employee can appeal the MSPB's decision to the U.S. Court of Appeals for the Federal Circuit.[27]

Conversely, the ICWPA provides no explicit mechanism for remedying for retaliation stemming from disclosure of an urgent concern to Congress; it merely prescribes the process through which such disclosures can be made and allows employees and contractors to then use those disclosure procedures to inform Congress of any resulting improper retaliation. Further, the ICWPA expressly states that Inspector General and agency head action taken pursuant to the ICWPA is not subject to judicial review, unlike retaliation claims under the WPA.[28] In comparing the ICWPA's protections against the WPA's, some commentators have questioned the ICWPA's effectiveness at protecting intelligence whistleblowers from improper retaliation.[29]

PRESIDENTIAL POLICY DIRECTIVE 19

President Obama issued PPD-19 on October 10, 2012, to ensure that IC employees can effectively report instances of waste, fraud, and abuse.[30] PPD-19 protects *employees* who engage in "protected disclosures" from certain types of adverse action by their employers. Thus, unlike the ICWPA, PPD-19's protections do not appear to extend to IC contractors. Under PPD-19, five types of disclosures fall under the umbrella of "protected disclosures." First, protected disclosures include employee disclosures to the agency Inspector General, Director of National Intelligence, IGIC, or supervisors within the employee's direct chain-of-command.[31] The employee must reasonably believe that disclosures to such persons evidence (1) a perceived violation of law, rule, or regulation; (2) gross mismanagement; (3) gross waste of funds; (4) abuse of authority; or (5) a specific and substantial threat to public health or safety.[32] Second, PPD-19 protects disclosures to congressional committees made pursuant to the ICWPA, discussed above.[33] Third, "protected disclosures" comprise any disclosure of a violation of PPD-19.[34] Fourth, protected disclosures include those made pursuant to an investigation or proceeding involving a violation of PPD-19.[35] Finally, the definition of "protected disclosures" generally includes disclosures to Inspectors General.[36]

Under PPD-19, intelligence agency[37] employees who make protected disclosures cannot consequently be subject to adverse personnel actions[38] or have their access to classified information negatively affected by an officer or employee of the agency.[39] PPD-19 required intelligence agencies to certify, within 270 days of its issuance, that they had internal procedures for reviewing allegations of wrongful personnel actions or impacts on access to classified information.[40] These procedures must provide for the protection of classified information and intelligence sources and methods.[41] PPD-19 requires that agency procedures permit agency Inspectors General to review employee allegations of adverse personnel action or improper restriction of access to classified information and recommend agency heads take corrective action if a violation of PPD-19 has occurred.[42] Such corrective action can include (but is not limited to) reinstatement, back pay, and attorney's fees.[43] Once an agency head receives an Inspector General's recommendation, PPD-19 requires he "carefully consider" the recommendation and findings and decide whether or not corrective action is appropriate.[44]

After employees exhaust the internal agency review process, PPD-19 allows them to request external review to the IGIC acting on behalf of the Director of National Intelligence.[45] Once such a request is made, the IGIC can, within his or her discretion, convene an external review panel.[46] Such a panel consists of the ICIG plus two Inspectors General that the ICIG chooses from the Departments of State, the Treasury, Defense, Justice, Energy, Homeland Security, or the CIA, exclusive of the Inspector General of the agency that internally reviewed the retaliation claim.[47] The panel then has 180 days to determine whether improper retaliation occurred.[48] If the panel concludes that such retaliation did happen, it can recommend that the agency head take corrective action, and the agency head must "carefully consider" this recommendation.[49] The agency head then has 90 days to inform the panel and the Director of National Intelligence of what, if any, action it takes.[50] The Director of National Intelligence must notify the President if the agency head does not tell the Director what action he takes within the allotted 90-day window.[51] PPD-19 further requires the IGIC to report annually all panel determinations and recommendations, along with agency head responses, to the Director of National Intelligence and, "as appropriate, to the relevant congressional committees."[52]

PPD-19 offers intelligence whistleblowers falling within its scope more protection against retaliation than the ICWPA. By allowing IC employees and contractors to disclose retaliation via adverse personnel action to congressional intelligence committees, the ICWPA purports to protect against only adverse personnel action; unlike PPD-19, it makes no mention of adverse security clearance determinations. Further, PPD-19, unlike the ICWPA, expressly prohibits retaliation against IC whistleblowers who make protected disclosures, whereas the ICWPA merely outlines the process through which such disclosures can be made.

Although PPD-19 offers intelligence whistleblowers more protection against retaliation than the ICWPA, it is unclear how effective PPD-19 will be in curbing such retaliation. Under PPD-19, the initial review of an improper retaliation allegation occurs within the agency wherein the whistleblower allegedly faced retaliation. This could raise questions regarding the initial review's impartiality, and thus effectiveness at achieving accurate results. Further, though PPD-19 appears to attempt to counteract impartiality in reviewing retaliation claims by creating an external review panel to whom such claims can eventually go, this external review panel cannot mandate that agency heads take corrective action after finding that impermissible retaliation occurred. Rather, this external review panel can only recommend that agency heads take corrective action. The agency head is then free to disregard the board's recommendation. Finally, as with all presidential policy directives or executive orders, President Obama (or any future Presidents) can revoke or modify it at any time.[53]

TITLE VI OF THE INTELLIGENCE AUTHORIZATION ACT FOR FY2015

On July 7, 2014, Congress enacted the Intelligence Authorization Act for FY2014,[54] which included protections for IC whistleblowers at Title VI of the act. Title VI seemingly codifies some of PPD-19's protections and, under specified circumstances, expands upon them. Like PPD-19, Title VI's protections extend only to *employees* of "covered intelligence community element[s],"[55] and therefore do not appear to apply to IC contractors.[56] Title VI's protections are bifurcated: it protects whistleblowers from retaliation in the form of both adverse personnel actions and adverse security clearance or information access determinations resulting from their making protected disclosures. Whether or not a disclosure is protected under Title VI depends on what is being disclosed to whom, and protected disclosures and enforcement mechanisms under the act differ in the context of retaliation via adverse personnel actions and adverse security clearance or information access determinations.

Protection from Adverse Personnel Actions

Under Title VI, disclosures for which an employee is protected against retaliation in the form of adverse personnel action include those made to (1) the Director of National Intelligence (or his or her designee); (2) the IGIC (or his or her designee); (3) the head of the employing agency (or his or her designee); (4) the employing agency's Inspector General; (5) congressional intelligence committees; or (6) a member of a congressional intelligence committee.[57] For Title VI to protect an employee against adverse personnel action, the disclosure must be of information that the employee reasonably believes evidences a violation of federal laws or regulations, mismanagement, waste of funds, abuse of authority, or a substantial and specific danger to public health or safety.[58] Title VI does not contain any mechanism to enforce its protection against retaliation by adverse personnel action; it merely prohibits agency employees from taking adverse personnel action against other employees who make protected disclosures.[59] Enforcement is expressly left to the President.[60] It is unclear whether the President will develop new enforcement procedures, or will utilize enforcement procedures that already exist (i.e., PPD-19's enforcement procedures).

Protection from Adverse Security Clearance and Information Access Determinations

Under Title VI, an IC employee cannot take adverse security clearance action against another employee, or restrict the other employee's access to classified information, because the employee made a protected disclosure.[61] The disclosures for which an employee cannot face adverse security clearance actions or access determinations differ from the disclosures for which an employee cannot face adverse personnel actions.[62] In the context of adverse security clearance actions or access determinations, Title VI's umbrella of protected disclosures includes a number of lawful communications. First, it includes communications to the Director of National Intelligence, agency head, or agency Inspector General (or their respective designees) that the employee reasonably believes evidences a violation of federal laws or regulations, gross mismanagement, waste of funds, abuse of authority, or a substantial and specific danger to public health or safety.[63] Second, it includes disclosures made in accordance with the procedures outlined in the ICWPA, discussed above.[64] Finally, Title VI protects disclosures made while exercising a legal right of appeal or complaint (including testimony in connection with someone else exercising such a right) or cooperating with an Inspector General.[65] However, disclosures within this third category fall within Title VI only if they do not result in the sharing of information that is classified under an executive order for national security reasons.[66]

Title VI's protections against adverse security or information access determinations also differ from its protections against adverse personnel actions because it provides mechanisms for enforcing the former; whereas enforcement of the latter is left to the President's discretion as mentioned above. Title VI directed the President to select, within 180 days of the statute's enactment (July 7, 2014), an agency or department responsible for ensuring that intelligence agencies have adequate procedural protections that they must follow before taking action that adversely affects an employee's security clearance or information access.[67] Within this time frame, the President must also select an agency or department responsible for developing procedures that agencies must follow for employee appeals of adverse security clearance or information access decisions to the ICIG or agency Inspector General.[68] Title VI permits an employee 90 days from the adverse security clearance or information determination to use these appeal procedures.[69]

The appeal procedures that must be established under Title VI must allow the ICIG or agency Inspector General to engage in a fact-finding investigation and report the investigation results to the agency head within 180 days of the employee's appeal.[70] During the investigation, the employee must be allowed, "to the fullest extent possible," to present relevant evidence.[71] The ICIG or agency Inspector General cannot find that a prohibited security clearance or information access determination occurred if the agency demonstrates that the employee's disclosure was not a contributing factor in the determination.[72] The agency can demonstrate such by establishing, by a preponderance of the evidence, that it would have taken the same action absent the employee's protected disclosures.[73] Under the preponderance of the evidence standard, it appears as though the agency must show that it is more likely than unlikely that the agency would have taken the same action against the employee absent the employee's disclosures.[74] In evaluating the agency's contributing factor evidence, Title VI requires the ICIG or agency Inspector General to afford the "utmost deference" to the agency's judgments regarding threats to national security.[75] If the ICIG or agency Inspector General determines that a prohibited security clearance or information access determination occurred and reports its determination to the agency head, the agency head "shall" take corrective action.[76]

If, however, the ICIG or agency Inspector General finds that no improper adverse security clearance or information access determination occurred, Title VI requires that the employee be given 60 days to externally appeal such a finding.[77] Title VI does not contain substantive requirements for this external appeal.[78] Rather, through the statute, Congress mandated that the Director of National Intelligence, in consultation with the Attorney General and the Secretary of Defense, develop and implement procedures for adjudicating external appeals.[79] As of this writing, the Director of National Intelligence does not appear to have developed these appeal procedures. Though Title VI does not contain substantive requirements for appeal procedures, it does require the Director of National Intelligence to inform the congressional intelligence committees when he issues an appeal order under the procedures that he develops.[80]

Title VI seemingly expands PPD-19's protections against retaliation in the form of adverse security clearance or information access determinations by introducing additional enforcement mechanisms. For example, Title VI requires adequate protections prior to adverse security clearance or information access determinations, where PPD-19 does not. However, Title VI does not appear to strengthen PPD-19's protections against retaliation in the form of adverse personnel action, as it leaves enforcement of such protections to the President.

End Notes

[1] P.L. 105-272, 112 Stat. 2396 (1998).

[2] OFFICE OF THE WHITE HOUSE PRESS SECRETARY, PRESIDENTIAL POLICY DIRECTIVE 19- PROTECTING WHISTLEBLOWERS WITH ACCESS TO CLASSIFIED INFORMATION (Oct. 10, 2012), hereinafter PPD-19.

[3] P.L. 113-126, 128 Stat. 1390, 1414 (2014).

[4] See S.Rept. 105-165, at 2 (1998).

[5] P.L. 101-12, 103 Stat. 16 (1989).

[6] The WPA, by its text, does not apply to employees of "the Federal Bureau of Investigation, the Central Intelligence Agency, the Defense Intelligence Agency, the National Geospatial-Intelligence Agency, the National Security Agency, the Office of the Director of National Intelligence, and the National Reconnaissance Office." 5 U.S.C. §2302(a)(2)(C).

[7] See P.L. 105-272, §701-02, 112 Stat. 2396, 2413 (1998).

[8] Id.

[9] The ICPWA provisions relating to employees and contractors of the Central Intelligence Agency (CIA) are at 50 U.S.C. §3517(d)(5). The parallel ICPWA provisions relating to employees and contractors of the Defense Intelligence Agency, National Imagery and Mapping Agency, National Reconnaissance Office, National Security Agency, Federal Bureau of Investigation, and any other agency that the President determines has the principal function of conducting foreign intelligence or counterintelligence activities are at 5 U.S.C. app. §8H.

[10] 50 U.S.C. §3517(d)(5)(A); 5 U.S.C. app. §8H(a)(1)(A), (B).

[11] 50 U.S.C. §3517(d)(5)(A); 5 U.S.C. app. §8H(a)(1)(A), (B).

[12] 50 U.S.C. §3517(d)(5)(g); 5 U.S.C. app. §8H(h)(1).

[13] 50 U.S.C. §3517(d)(5)(g)(i)(I); 5 U.S.C. app. §8H(h)(1)(A). It cannot, however, be a difference in opinion on public policy matters. 50 U.S.C. §3517(d)(5)(g)(i)(I); 5 U.S.C. app. §8H(h)(1)(A)

[14] 50 U.S.C. §3517(d)(5)(g)(i)(II); 5 U.S.C. app. §8H(h)(1)(B).

[15] 50 U.S.C. §3517(d)(5)(g)(i)(III); 5 U.S.C. app. §8H(h)(1)(C).

[16] See 50 U.S.C. §3517(d)(5)(A); see also 5 U.S.C. app. §8H(a)(1)(A), (B).

[17] 50 U.S.C. §3517(d)(5)(A); 5 U.S.C. app. §8H(a)(1)(A), (B). Inspectors General are generally intended to provide independent, objective audits and investigations of agency operations, among other things. See 50 U.S.C. §3517(a); see also 5 U.S.C. app. §2. The Inspector General of the IC is responsible for, among other things, conducting independent investigations, inspections, and audits of programs and activities that the Director of National Intelligence is responsible for administering. 50 U.S.C. §3033(b).

[18] 50 U.S.C. §3517(d)(5)(B); 5 U.S.C. app. §8H(b).

[19] 50 U.S.C. §3517(d)(5)(B); 5 U.S.C. app. §8H(b).

[20] 50 U.S.C. §3517(d)(5)(C); 5 U.S.C. app. §8H(c). "Congressional intelligence committees" refers to the Senate Select Committee on Intelligence and the House Permanent Select Committee on Intelligence. 50 U.S.C. §3517(a)(4); 5 U.S.C. app. §8H(h)(2).

[21] 50 U.S.C. §3517(d)(5)(D)(i); 5 U.S.C. app. §8H(d)(1). When an employee contacts a committee member or employee directly, the committee member or employee "receives [the] complaint or information ... in that member or employee's official capacity as a member or employee of that committee." 50 U.S.C. §3517(d)(5)(D)(iii); 5 U.S.C. app. §8H(d)(3).

[22] 50 U.S.C. §3517(d)(5)(D)(ii)(I); 5 U.S.C. app. §8H(d)(2)(A).

[23] 50 U.S.C. §3517(d)(5)(D)(ii)(II); 5 U.S.C. app. §8H(d)(2)(B).

[24] The WPA, by its text, does not apply to employees of "the Federal Bureau of Investigation, the Central Intelligence Agency, the Defense Intelligence Agency, the National Geospatial-Intelligence Agency, the National Security Agency, the Office of the Director of National Intelligence, and the National Reconnaissance Office." 5 U.S.C. §2302(a)(2)(C).

[25] 5 U.S.C. §1221.

[26] Id. at (g)(1)(A). The MSPB is an independent, quasi-judicial government agency that, among other things, "adjudicat[es] Federal employee appeals of agency personnel actions ..." 5 C.F.R. §1200.1.

[27] See 5 U.S.C. §1214(c).

[28] 50 U.S.C. §3517(d)(5)(F); 5 U.S.C. app. §8H(f).

[29] See, e.g., Mary-Rose Papandrea, Leaker Traitor Whistleblower Spy: National Security Leaks and the First Amendment, 94 B.U. L. Rev. 449, 493 (2014) (observing that "... the ICWPA arguably fails to provide any real protection ..."); See Richard Moberly, Whistleblowers and the Obama Presidency: the National Security Dilemma, 16 Emp. Rts. & Emp. Pol'y J. 51, 109 (2012) (detailing perceived gaps in the protections that the ICWPA affords intelligence whistleblowers).

[30] PPD-19 at 1. Presidential policy directives are binding on executive agencies and, in practice, can be equivalent to executive orders. See Ctr. for Effective Gov't v. Department of State, No. 13-0414, 2013 WL 6641262, at *2, n. 3 (D.D.C. Dec. 17, 2013) ("even though issued as a directive, the PPD-6 carries the force of law as policy guidance to be implemented by recipient agencies, and it is the functional equivalent of an Executive Order.").

[31] PPD-19 at 7.

[32] Id.

[33] See id.

[34] Id.

[35] Id. at 8.

[36] Id.

[37] More specifically, PPD-19 applies to so-called "Covered Agenc[ies]", which it defines as an executive department or independent establishment that contains an "Intelligence Community Element," including the Central Intelligence Agency, National Security Agency, Defense Intelligence Agency, National Geospatial-Intelligence Agency, National Reconnaissance Office, and any other agency that the President determines has as its principal function the conduct of foreign intelligence or counterintelligence activities. Id. at 6. The directive explicitly states that the Federal Bureau of Investigations is not a "Covered Agency." Id.

[38] Prohibited personnel actions include, but are not limited to, transfer, reassignment, demotion, suspension, termination, and negative decisions regarding pay or benefits. Id.

[39] Id. at 2-3.

[40] Id. PPD-19 mandates that such review processes apply to any actions arising after the date on which the intelligence agency head certifies the agency review process. Id.

[41] Id.

[42] Id.

[43] Id.

[44] Id.

[45] Id. at 4. The Director of National Intelligence is a presidential appointee "subject to the authority, direction, and control of the President" who, among other things, advises the President, National Security Council, and Homeland Security Council on intelligence matters related to national security. 50 U.S.C. §3023.

[46] PPD-19 at 4.

[47] Id.

[48] Id.

[49] Id.

[50] Id.

[51] Id.

[52] Id.

[53] See CRS Report RS20846, Executive Orders: Issuance, Modification, and Revocation, by Vivian S. Chu and Todd Garvey.

[54] P.L. 113-126, 128 Stat. 1390 (2014).

[55] Covered agencies include the Central Intelligence Agency, National Geospatial-Intelligence Agency, Office of the Director of National Intelligence, Defense Intelligence Agency, National Security Agency, and the National Reconnaissance Office. 50 U.S.C. §3234(a)(2).

[56] See 50 U.S.C. §3234(b); 50 U.S.C. §3341(j)(1).

[57] 50 U.S.C. §3234(b).

[58] Id.

[59] 50 U.S.C. §3234(b).

[60] 50 U.S.C. §3234(c).

[61] 50 U.S.C. §3341(j)(1).

[62] Compare 50 U.S.C. §3234(b) with 50 U.S.C. §3341(j)(1)(A)-(D).

[63] 50 U.S.C. §3341(j)(1)(A),(B).

[64] 50 U.S.C. §3341(j)(1)(C).

[65] 50 U.S.C. §3341(j)(1)(D).

[66] Id.

[67] 50 U.S.C. §3341(b)(7)(B).

[68] 50 U.S.C. §3341(b)(7)(A); P.L. 113-126, §602(a)(2), 128 Stat. 1390, 1416-17 (2014).

[69] 50 U.S.C. §3341(j)(4)(A).

[70] P.L. 113-126, §602(a)(2), 128 Stat. 1390, 1416-17 (2014).

[71] Id.

[72] 50 U.S.C. §3341(j)(4)(C).

[73] Id.

[74] See Concrete Pipe and Prods. of Cal v. Constr. Laborers Pension Trust of S. Cal., 508 U.S. 602, 622 (observing that showing a fact by a preponderance of the evidence "simply requires the trier of fact to believe that the existence of a fact is more probable than its nonexistence ...") (internal quotations omitted).

[75] Id.

[76] 50 U.S.C. §3341(j)(4)(B). This corrective action must, as "nearly as practicable and reasonable," put the employee in the position he would have been in but-for the prohibited retaliation and can include compensatory damages of up to $300,000. Id.

[77] 50 U.S.C. §3341(j)(5)(A).

[78] See id.

[79] 50 U.S.C. §3341(j)(5)(B).

[80] 50 U.S.C. §3341(j)(5)(C).

In: Whistleblowers:
Editor: Andre Pope

ISBN: 978-1-63482-290-9

Chapter 2

WHISTLEBLOWER PROTECTIONS UNDER FEDERAL LAW: AN OVERVIEW*

Jon O. Shimabukuro and L. Paige Whitaker

SUMMARY

Legal protections for employees who report illegal misconduct by their employers have increased dramatically since the late 1970s when such protections were first adopted for federal employees in the Civil Service Reform Act of 1978. Since that time, with the enactment of the Whistleblower Protection Act of 1989, Congress has expanded such protections for federal employees. Congress has also established whistleblower protections for individuals in certain private-sector employment through the adoption of whistleblower provisions in at least 18 federal statutes. Among these statutes is the Sarbanes-Oxley Act, the FDA Food Safety Modernization Act, and the Dodd-Frank Wall Street Reform and Consumer Protection Act (Dodd-Frank Act).

In general, claims for relief under the 18 federal statutes follow a similar pattern. Complaints are typically filed with the Secretary of Labor, and an investigation is conducted. Following the investigation, an order is issued by the Secretary, and a party aggrieved by the order is generally permitted to appeal the Secretary's order to a federal court. However, because 18 different statutes are involved in prescribing

---

* This is an edited, reformatted and augmented version of a Congressional Research Service publication, CRS Report for Congress R42727, from www.crs.gov, prepared for Members and Committees of Congress, dated September 13, 2012.

whistleblower protections, some notable differences exist. For example, under the Department of Defense Authorization Act of 1987, individuals employed by defense contractors who engage in whistleblowing activities file complaints with the Inspector General rather than the Secretary of Labor. Under some of the statutes, including the Commercial Motor Vehicle Safety Act and the Dodd-Frank Act, the Secretary's preliminary order will become a final order if no objections are filed within a prescribed time period.

This report provides an overview of key aspects of the 18 selected federal statutes applicable to individuals in certain private-sector industries. It focuses on the protections provided to employees who believe they have been subject to retaliation, rather than on how or where alleged misconduct should be disclosed. In addition, the report also includes an overview of the Whistleblower Protection Act. While state law may also provide whistleblower protections for employees, this report focuses only on the aforementioned federal statutory provisions.

INTRODUCTION

Legal protections for employees who report illegal misconduct by their employers have increased dramatically since the late 1970s when such protections were first adopted for federal employees in the Civil Service Reform Act of 1978. Since that time, with the enactment of the Whistleblower Protection Act of 1989, as amended, Congress has expanded such protections for federal employees. Congress has also established whistleblower protections for individuals in certain private-sector employment through the adoption of whistleblower provisions in at least 18 other industry-specific federal statutes. For example, in 2002, Congress passed the Sarbanes-Oxley Act (SOX) in response to corporate scandals that occurred in the late 1990s and early 2000s. SOX established new civil protections for employees who report concerns about alleged fraud upon shareholders. More recently, Congress passed the FDA Food Safety Modernization Act (FDA Modernization Act), which prohibits entities engaged in food manufacturing, processing, and related activities from discharging or otherwise discriminating against an employee for providing information related to any violation or act that the employee reasonably believes to be a violation of the Federal Food, Drug, and Cosmetic Act.[1]

This report provides an overview of whistleblower provisions in 19 selected federal statutes. While state law may also provide whistleblower protections for employees, this report focuses on relevant federal statutory provisions. The report does not discuss the qui tam and whistleblower provisions of the False Claims Act that permit private citizens with knowledge of fraud against the federal government to sue on its behalf and receive a portion of the recovered proceeds.

CLEAN AIR ACT (CAA)

The CAA prohibits an employer from discharging or otherwise discriminating against any employee with respect to his or her compensation, terms, conditions, or privileges of employment because the employee (1) commenced or is about to commence a proceeding under the CAA or a proceeding for the administration or enforcement of any requirement imposed by the CAA; (2) testified or is about to testify in any such proceeding; or (3) assisted or participated or is about to assist or participate in any manner in such a proceeding.[2] Any employee who believes that he or she has been discharged or otherwise discriminated against in violation of the CAA may, within 30 days after such violation occurs, file a complaint with the Secretary of Labor. Upon receipt of the complaint, the Secretary will conduct an investigation and within 30 days of the receipt of such complaint, shall notify the complainant and the alleged violator with the results of the investigation. Within 90 days of receipt of the complaint, the Secretary shall issue an order either providing relief or denying the complaint. If the Secretary determines that a violation has occurred, the Secretary will order the person who committed such violation to (1) take affirmative action to abate the violation, and (2) reinstate the complainant to his or her former position with compensation, including back pay, terms, conditions, and privileges of employment. The Secretary may order the payment of compensatory damages to the complainant. If an order is issued, at the request of the complainant, the Secretary will assess against the person against whom the order is issued a sum equal to the aggregate amount of all costs and expenses, including attorneys' and expert witness fees, reasonably incurred by the complainant in bringing the complaint.[3]

Any person adversely affected or aggrieved by an order issued under the CAA's whistleblower provisions may obtain review of the order in the U.S. court of appeals for the circuit in which the violation allegedly occurred. The petition for review must be filed within 60 days from the issuance of the Secretary's order, and the commencement of proceedings shall not, unless ordered by the court, operate as a stay of the Secretary's order.

The Secretary may file a civil action in the U.S. district court in which the violation occurred when a person has failed to comply with an order.

An order by the Secretary is not subject to judicial review in any criminal or other civil proceeding. When a person has failed to comply with an order, the Secretary may file a civil action in the U.S. district court in which the violation occurred and the district courts shall have jurisdiction to grant all appropriate relief, including injunctive relief, as well as compensatory and exemplary damages.[4] Any person on whose behalf an order was issued may commence a civil action against the person to whom such order was issued to require compliance, and the appropriate U.S. district court shall have jurisdiction, without regard to the amount in controversy or citizenship of the parties. In issuing any final order, the court may award costs of litigation, including reasonable attorney and expert witness fees, to any party whenever the court determines it is appropriate.[5]

COMMERCIAL MOTOR VEHICLE SAFETY ACT (CMVSA)

The CMVSA prohibits employers from discharging, disciplining, or discriminating against an employee regarding pay, terms, or privileges of employment because the employee filed a complaint or instituted a proceeding related to a violation of a commercial motor vehicle safety regulation, standard, or order, or has testified or will testify in such proceeding. Additionally, any employee who refuses to operate a vehicle because the operation violates a regulation, standard, or order related to commercial motor vehicle safety or health, or has a reasonable apprehension of serious injury because of the vehicle's unsafe condition, is likewise protected from such retaliatory action.[6]

An employee alleging discharge, discipline, or discrimination in violation of the CMVSA may file a complaint with the Secretary of Labor within 180 days after the alleged violation occurred. Within 60 days of receiving the complaint, the Secretary will conduct an investigation, decide whether the complaint has merit, and notify the complainant and the person alleged to have committed the violation of the findings. If the Secretary determines that it is reasonable to believe that the violation occurred, the Secretary will include in the findings a preliminary order for relief. Within 30 days of receiving notice of the Secretary's findings, the complainant and person alleged to have committed the violation may file objections to the findings or preliminary order and request a hearing on the record, although the filing of objections does not stay a reinstatement ordered in the preliminary order. If a hearing is not requested within 30 days, the preliminary order is final and not subject to judicial review. A hearing shall be conducted expeditiously, and not later than 120 days after the end of the hearing, the Secretary will issue a final order. Before the final order is issued, the proceeding may be ended by settlement agreement by the Secretary, the complainant, and the person alleged to have committed the violation. If the Secretary determines that a violation of this provision occurred, he or she can order the person alleged to have committed the violation to (1) take affirmative action to abate the violation; (2) reinstate the complainant to the former position with the same pay and terms and privileges of employment; and (3) pay compensatory damages, including back pay. Upon request by the complainant, the Secretary may assess against the person against whom the order is issued the costs, including attorneys' fees, reasonably incurred by the complainant in bringing the complaint.[7]

Within 60 days after an order is issued, a person adversely affected may file a petition for review in the U.S. court of appeals for the circuit in which the violation occurred or the person resided on the date of the violation. The review will be heard and decided expeditiously and an order is not subject to judicial review in a criminal or other civil proceeding. If a person fails to comply with an order issued under this provision, the Secretary will bring a civil action to enforce the order in the U.S. district court for the judicial district in which the violation occurred.[8]

COMPREHENSIVE ENVIRONMENTAL RESPONSE COMPENSATION AND LIABILITY ACT OF 1980 (CERCLA)

CERCLA, also known as the "Superfund" Act, prohibits an employer from firing or in any other way discriminating against, or causing to be fired or discriminated against, any employee because that employee provided information to a state or the federal government; filed, instituted, or caused to be filed or instituted any proceeding under the statute; or has testified or will testify in a proceeding resulting from the administration or enforcement of the statute.[9] Any employee who believes that he or she has been terminated or otherwise discriminated against by any person in violation of CERCLA's whistleblower provisions may, within 30 days, apply to the Secretary of Labor for a review of the termination or alleged discrimination. Upon receipt of such application, the Secretary will institute an investigation and upon receiving the investigation report, make findings of fact. If the Secretary finds that a violation occurred, she will issue a decision, incorporating an order, requiring the party committing the violation to take such affirmative action to abate the violation as the Secretary deems appropriate, including reinstatement to the former position with compensation. If she finds no violation, the Secretary will issue an order denying the application. An order issued by the Secretary is subject to judicial review.[10] When an order is issued under this provision, at the request of the applicant, a sum equal to the aggregate amount of all costs and expenses, including attorneys' fees, will be assessed against the person committing such violation.[11]

> Defense contractor employees who engage in whistleblowing activities file complaints with the Inspector General (IG) rather than the Secretary of Labor.

DEPARTMENT OF DEFENSE AUTHORIZATION ACT OF 1987

The Department of Defense Authorization Act of 1987 prohibits defense contractors from discharging, demoting, or otherwise discriminating against an employee as a reprisal for disclosing to a Member of Congress, an authorized official of an agency, or the Department of Justice information relating to a substantial violation of law related to a contract, including the competition for or negotiation of a contract.[12] Any person who believes that he or she has been subject to a prohibited reprisal may submit a complaint to the Inspector General (IG), who is required to investigate the complaint unless the IG determines that the complaint is frivolous. Upon completion of the investigation, the IG will submit a report of the findings of the investigation to the individual, relevant contractor, and the head of the agency.[13] If the agency head determines that a contractor has subjected a person to a prohibited reprisal, the agency head may take one or more of the following actions: (1) order the contractor to abate the reprisal; (2) order the contractor to reinstate the person to the position that the person held before the reprisal, together with compensation, including back pay, employment benefits, and other applicable terms and conditions of employment; (3) order the contractor to pay the complainant an amount equal to the aggregate amount of all costs and expenses, including attorneys' and expert witnesses' fees, that were reasonably incurred by the complainant.[14] If a person fails to comply with such an order, the agency head will file an action for enforcement in the U.S. district court for the district in which the reprisal occurred. The court may grant appropriate relief, including injunctive relief, as well as compensatory and exemplary damages.[15] Within 60 days after the order is issued, any person adversely affected or aggrieved by such an order may obtain review in the U.S. court of appeals for a circuit in which the reprisal occurred.[16]

DODD-FRANK WALL STREET REFORM AND CONSUMER PROTECTION ACT (DODD-FRANK ACT)

The Dodd-Frank Act established several new whistleblower protections for individuals employed in the financial services industry. Section 748 of the Dodd-Frank Act, for example, amended the Commodity Exchange Act (CEA) to prohibit employers from discharging or otherwise discriminating against an individual for providing information related to a violation of the CEA to the Commodity Futures Trading Commission (CFTC) or for assisting in any investigation or judicial or administrative action of the CFTC based upon or related to such information. An individual who alleges a termination or other discrimination in violation of the CEA provisions may bring an action in the appropriate district court of the United States. If the individual is a federal employee, he or she must bring the action in accordance with Section 1221 of Title 5, U.S. Code.[17] An individual who prevails in a whistleblower action will be awarded reinstatement, back pay with interest, and compensation for any special damages sustained as result of the discharge or discrimination, including litigation costs and reasonable attorney's fees.

An individual who prevails in an action under Section 21F will be awarded two times the amount of back pay otherwise owed.

Section 922 of the Dodd-Frank Act amended the Securities Exchange Act of 1934 to add a new Section 21F that prohibits employers from discharging or otherwise discriminating against an individual for (1) providing information related to a violation of the securities laws to the Securities and Exchange Commission (SEC); (2) initiating, testifying in, or assisting in any investigation or judicial or administrative action of the SEC based upon or related to such information;or (3) making disclosures that are required by SOX, the Securities Exchange Act of 1934, or any other law subject to the

SEC's jurisdiction. An individual who alleges a termination or other discrimination in violation of these provisions may bring an action in the appropriate district court of the United States. An individual who prevails in a whistleblower action under Section 21F will be awarded reinstatement, two times the amount of back pay otherwise owed to the individual, with interest, and compensation for litigation costs, expert witness fees, and reasonable expenses.

Section 1057 of the Dodd-Frank Act prohibits employers engaged in providing consumer financial products or services, and employers that provide a material service in connection with the provision of such products or services, from terminating or in any other way discriminating against a covered employee because the employee has (1) provided, caused to be provided, or is about to provide or cause to be provided, information relating to a violation of Title X of the Dodd-Frank Act or any other provision of law that is subject to the jurisdiction of the Bureau of Consumer Financial Protection (Bureau) to the employer, the Bureau, or a state, local, or federal government authority or law enforcement agency; (2) testified or will testify in any proceeding resulting from the administration or enforcement of Title X of the Dodd-Frank Act or any other provision of law that is subject to the jurisdiction of the Bureau; (3) filed, instituted, or caused to be filed or instituted any proceeding under any federal consumer financial law; or (4) objected to or refused to participate in any activity that the employee reasonably believed to be in violation of any law subject to the jurisdiction of, or enforceable by, the Bureau.[18]

An employee who believes that he or she has been discharged or otherwise discriminated against in violation of the Section 1057 whistleblower provisions may file a complaint with the Secretary of Labor within 180 days of the alleged violation. Within 60 days after receiving the complaint, the Secretary will initiate an investigation and determine whether there is reasonable cause to believe that the complaint has merit. The Secretary will notify the complainant and the person alleged to have committed the violation of her determination in writing. If the Secretary concludes that there is reasonable cause to believe that a violation has occurred, she will also issue a preliminary order that provides relief. Either party may file objections to the Secretary's findings or order and request a hearing within 30 days after receiving her notification. If a hearing is not requested in the 30-day period, the preliminary order shall be deemed a final order that is not subject to judicial review.[19]

If a hearing is conducted, the Secretary is required to issue a final order providing relief or denying the complaint within 120 days after the date of the hearing's conclusion. If the Secretary determines that a violation has occurred, she may order the person who committed the violation to take affirmative action to abate the violation, order the reinstatement of the complainant to his or her former position with compensation, including back pay, and order the payment of compensatory damages. At the request of the complainant, the Secretary will also assess against the person who committed the violation a sum equal to the aggregate amount of all legal costs and expenses reasonably incurred. Any person adversely affected or aggrieved by a final order may seek review of the order in the U.S. court of appeals for the circuit in which the violation allegedly occurred or the circuit in which the complainant resided on the date of such violation. If the Secretary fails to issue a timely final order, the complainant may seek *de novo* review in the appropriate district court of the United States having jurisdiction.

ENERGY REORGANIZATION ACT OF 1974 (ERA)

The ERA prohibits employers from discharging or otherwise discriminating against any employee who (1) notified his or her employer of an alleged violation of the ERA or the Atomic Energy Act of 1954 (AEA); (2) refused to engage in any unlawful practice under the ERA or AEA, if the employee identified the alleged illegality to the employer; (3) testified before Congress or at any federal or state proceeding regarding any provision of the ERA or AEA; (4) commenced a proceeding under the ERA or AEA; (5) testified or is about to testify in any such proceeding; or (6) assisted or participated or is about to assist or participate in a proceeding to carry out the purposes of the ERA or AEA.[20] Any employee who believes that he or she has been discharged or otherwise discriminated against in violation of the ERA's whistleblower provisions may, within 180 days after such violation occurs, file a complaint with the Secretary of Labor alleging such discharge or discrimination. Upon receipt of a complaint, the Secretary will complete an investigation within 30 days. Within 90 days of receiving the complaint, the Secretary will, unless the proceeding is terminated due to a settlement, issue an order either providing relief or denying the complaint. Upon the conclusion of a public hearing and the issuance of a recommended decision that the complaint has merit, the Secretary will issue a preliminary order providing relief, but may not order compensatory damages pending a final order.

> The Secretary will dismiss a complaint and not conduct an investigation unless the complainant has made a prima facie showing that the protected action was a contributing factor in the alleged unfavorable personnel action.

If the Secretary determines that a violation has occurred, she will order the person who committed such violation to (1) take affirmative action to abate the violation, and (2) reinstate the complainant to his former position together with compensation, including back pay, terms, conditions, and privileges of his or her employment. The Secretary may order the person who committed the violation to provide compensatory damages to the complainant. If an order is issued, the Secretary, at the request of the complainant, will assess a sum equal to the aggregate amount of all costs and expenses, including attorneys' and expert witness fees, reasonably incurred by the complainant. The Secretary will dismiss a complaint and not conduct an investigation unless the complainant has made a prima facie showing that the protected action by the employee was a contributing factor in the unfavorable personnel action alleged in the complaint. Notwithstanding a finding by the Secretary that the complainant has made the required prima facie showing, no investigation shall be conducted if the employer demonstrates, by clear and convincing evidence, that it would have taken the same unfavorable personnel action in the absence of such behavior. Relief may not be ordered if the employer demonstrates by clear and convincing evidence that it would have taken the same unfavorable personnel action in the absence of such behavior.[21]

Any person adversely affected by an order issued under the ERA's whistleblower provisions may obtain review of the order in the U.S. court of appeals for the circuit in which the violation allegedly occurred. A petition for review must be filed within 60 days of the issuance of the Secretary's order. Review shall conform to chapter 7 of Title 5, U.S. Code, and the commencement of proceedings under this provision shall not, unless ordered by the court, operate as a stay of the Secretary's order.

An order by the Secretary shall not be subject to judicial review in any criminal or other civil proceeding. Whenever a person fails to comply with an order issued under this provision, the Secretary may file a civil action in the U.S. district court for the district in which the violation occurred. In actions brought under this provision, the district courts shall have jurisdiction to grant all appropriate relief, including injunctive relief and compensatory and exemplary damages. Any person on whose behalf an order was issued may commence a civil action against the person to whom such order was issued to require compliance with such order; the appropriate U.S. district court shall have jurisdiction, without regard to the amount in controversy or citizenship of the parties; and in issuing any final order under this subsection, the court may award costs of litigation, including reasonable attorney and expert witness fees.[22]

FAIR LABOR STANDARDS ACT OF 1938 (FLSA)

The FLSA prohibits employers from discharging or otherwise discriminating against an employee because such employee filed a complaint or instituted any proceeding under the statute, testified or is about to testify in any such proceeding, or served or is about to serve on an industry committee.[23] Employers who willfully violate the FLSA's anti-retaliation provisions may be fined up to $10,000 and imprisoned up to six months. Employers who retaliate against employees in violation of this provision shall be liable for legal and equitable relief, including, without limitation, reinstatement, the payment of lost wages, and an additional equal amount as liquidated damages. An action may be maintained against any employer, including a public agency, in any federal or state court of competent jurisdiction by any one or more employees. The court shall, in addition to any judgment awarded, allow reasonable attorneys' fees to be paid to the plaintiff, as well as the costs of the action. An employee loses his or her right to file a complaint under this provision once the Secretary of Labor files a complaint against the employer.[24]

> Willful violations of the FLSA's anti-retaliation provisions could result in fines up to $10,000 and imprisonment up to six months.

FDA FOOD SAFETY MODERNIZATION ACT (FDA MODERNIZATION ACT)

The FDA Modernization Act amended the Federal Food, Drug, and Cosmetic Act to prohibit an entity engaged in the manufacture, processing, packing, transporting, distribution, reception, holding, or importation of food from discharging or otherwise discriminating against an employee with respect to the individual's compensation, terms, conditions, or privileges of employment because the employee (1) provided, caused to be provided, or is about to provide or cause to be provided information relating to a violation of the Federal Food, Drug, and Cosmetic Act to the employer, the federal government, or the attorney general of a state; (2) testified or is about to testify in a proceeding concerning the violation; (3) assisted or participated or is about to assist or participate in a proceeding concerning the violation; or (4) objected to, or refused to participate in any activity that the employee believed to be in violation of the Federal Food, Drug, and Cosmetic Act.[25]

An individual who believes that he or she has been discharged or otherwise discriminated against in violation of the relevant whistleblower provisions may file a complaint with the Secretary of Labor within 180 days after the date on which the violation occurs.[26] Within 60 days of receiving the complaint, the Secretary will initiate an investigation and determine whether there is reasonable cause to believe that the complaint has merit. If the Secretary determines that reasonable cause exists, she will accompany her findings with a preliminary order that requires the person who committed the violation to take affirmative action to abate the violation, to reinstate the complainant to his or her former position with compensation, and to provide compensatory damages. The person alleged to have committed the violation or the complainant may file objections to the findings or the preliminary order and request a hearing. A final order must be issued by the Secretary within 120 days after the date of the hearing's conclusion. If the Secretary fails to issue a timely final decision, the complainant may seek *de novo* review in the appropriate district court of the United States with jurisdiction.

FEDERAL MINE SAFETY AND HEALTH ACT (FMSHA)

The FMSHA prohibits an employer from discharging an employee or applicant for employment because the individual (1) filed or made a complaint under or related to the FMSHA; (2) is the subject of medical evaluations and potential transfer; (3) instituted or testified in any proceeding under or related to the FMSHA; or (4) exercised any statutory right afforded by the FMSHA.[27] Employees and applicants who believe that they have been discharged, interfered with, or otherwise discriminated against in violation of this prohibition may file a complaint with the Secretary of Labor within 60 days after the alleged violation. Upon receipt of the complaint, the Secretary will forward a copy to the respondent and within 15 days of receiving the complaint, the Secretary will institute an investigation as she deems appropriate. If the Secretary determines that the complaint was not brought frivolously, the Federal Mine Safety and Health Review Commission will order the immediate reinstatement of the miner pending a final order. If the Secretary determines that the FMSHA's whistleblower provisions have been violated, she will immediately file a complaint with the Commission, with service upon the alleged violator and miner, proposing an order granting appropriate relief. The Commission shall afford an opportunity for a hearing and shall issue an order, affirming, modifying, or vacating the Secretary's proposed order, or directing other appropriate relief. The Commission retains the authority to require a person committing a violation to abate the violation as the Commission deems appropriate, including the rehiring or reinstatement of the miner to his or her former position with back pay and interest.[28]

If the Secretary determines that the complaint was not brought frivolously, the Federal Mine Safety and Health Review Commission will order the immediate reinstatement of the miner pending final order.

Within 90 days of receiving a complaint, the Secretary will notify the miner about whether a violation occurred. If the Secretary determines that the FMSHA's whistleblower provisions were violated, the complainant shall have the right to file an action in his or her own behalf before the Commission. The Commission shall afford an opportunity for a hearing and shall issue an order, granting such relief as it deems appropriate. Whenever an order is issued sustaining a complainant's charges, a sum equal to the aggregate amount of all costs and expenses, including attorneys' fees, will be assessed against the person who committed the violation. Any person adversely affected by such an order may obtain review in any U.S. court of appeals for the circuit in which the violation is alleged to have occurred or in the U.S. Court of Appeals for the D.C. Circuit.[29]

FEDERAL WATER POLLUTION CONTROL ACT OF 1972 (FWPCA)

The FWPCA prohibits an employer from firing or otherwise discriminating against an employee, or causing such firing or discrimination, because the employee has filed, instituted, or caused to be filed or instituted any proceeding under the FWPCA, or has testified or is about to testify in any proceeding resulting from the administration or enforcement of the FWPCA.[30]

Any employee who believes that he or she has been fired or discriminated against in violation of this provision may, within 30 days after such alleged violation occurs, apply to the Secretary of Labor for a review. Upon receipt of such application, the Secretary will institute an investigation as he or she deems appropriate. Upon receiving the report of such investigation, the Secretary will make findings of fact; if she finds that such violation did occur, the Secretary will issue a decision, incorporating an order and findings, requiring the party committing such violation to take such affirmative action to abate the violation, including the rehiring or reinstatement of the employee with compensation. If the Secretary finds that there was no such violation, she will issue an order denying the application; such order shall be subject to judicial review in the same manner as orders and decisions are subject to judicial review under 33 U.S.C. §§ 1251 *et seq.* Whenever an order is issued, at the request of the applicant, a sum equal to the aggregate amount of all costs and expenses, including attorneys' fees, determined to have been reasonably incurred by the applicant, will be assessed against the person committing the violation.

Longshore and Harbor Workers' Compensation Act (LHWCA)

The LHWCA prohibits an employer from discharging or otherwise discriminating against an employee who claims or attempts to claim compensation from the employer, or testifies or is about to testify against the employer in a proceeding under the statute. Any employer who violates this provision will be liable for a penalty of not less than $1,000 nor more than $5,000. If such penalties are not paid, they may be recovered in a civil action brought in the appropriate U.S. district court.

> If the employee ceases to be qualified to perform the duties of employment, the employee will not be restored to his or her position and will not be compensated for any wage loss.

Any employee that is discriminated against under the statute's whistleblower provisions shall be restored to his or her employment and shall be compensated for any loss of wages arising from the discrimination, provided that if the employee ceases to be qualified to perform the duties of employment, he or she shall not be entitled to such restoration and compensation. The employer and not his insurance carrier shall be liable for such penalties and payments, and any provision in an insurance policy undertaking to relieve the employer from the liability for such penalties and payments shall be void.[31]

MIGRANT AND SEASONAL AGRICULTURAL WORKER PROTECTION ACT (MSAWPA)

The MSAWPA prohibits employers from intimidating, threatening, restraining, coercing, blacklisting, discharging, or in any manner discriminating against any migrant or seasonal agricultural worker because such worker has, with just cause, filed a complaint or instituted, or caused to be instituted, any proceeding under the statute's anti-retaliation provisions. Additionally, any employee who has testified or is about to testify in any such proceeding or justifiably exercises any right or protection afforded by MSAWPA is protected from retaliatory action.[32] An employee who believes, with just cause, that he or she has been discriminated against in violation of the relevant provisions may file a complaint with the Secretary of Labor within 180 days of the violation. As she deems appropriate, the Secretary will institute an investigation and, upon determining that a violation has occurred, will bring an action in any appropriate U.S. district court. In any such action, the U.S. district court will have jurisdiction, for cause shown, to restrain the violation and order all appropriate relief, including reinstatement with back pay or damages.[33]

OCCUPATIONAL SAFETY AND HEALTH ACT OF 1970 (OSH ACT)

The OSH Act prohibits employers from discharging or in any manner discriminating against an employee because such employee filed a complaint or instituted or caused to be instituted a proceeding under the OSH Act, or is about to testify in any such proceeding. Additionally, any employee who has testified or is about to testify in any such proceeding or exercises any right or protection afforded by the OSH Act is protected from retaliatory action. An employee who believes that he or she has been discharged or otherwise discriminated against in violation of the OSH Act may file a complaint with the Secretary of Labor alleging such discrimination within 30 days. Upon receipt of such complaint, the Secretary will institute an investigation as she deems appropriate. If the Secretary determines that a violation has occurred, she will bring an action in any appropriate U.S. district court. The U.S. district court shall have jurisdiction, for cause shown, to restrain the violation and order all appropriate relief including reinstatement with back pay.[34]

SAFE DRINKING WATER ACT (SDWA)

The SDWA prohibits employers from firing, or in any other way discriminating against, or causing to be fired or discriminated against, any employee because such employee filed, instituted, or caused to be filed or instituted any proceeding under the SDWA or has testified or is about to testify in any proceeding resulting from the administration or enforcement of the SDWA. Any employee who believes that he or she has been fired or otherwise discriminated against in violation of the SDWA may, within 30 days after such alleged violation occurs, apply to the Secretary of Labor for a review. Upon receipt of such application, the Secretary will initiate an investigation as she deems appropriate. Upon receiving the report of such investigation, the Secretary will make findings of fact; if she finds that such violation did occur, the Secretary will issue a decision, incorporating an order and findings, requiring the party committing such violation to take such affirmative action to abate the violation, including, the rehiring or reinstatement of the employee with compensation. If the Secretary finds that there was no such violation, she will issue an order denying the application; such order is subject to judicial review in the same manner as orders and decisions are subject to judicial review under 42 U.S.C. §§ 6901 *et seq.* Whenever an order is issued, at the request of the applicant, a sum equal to the aggregate amount of all costs and expenses, including attorneys' fees, determined to have been reasonably incurred by the applicant, shall be assessed against the person who committed the violation.[35]

Any employee or employer adversely affected or aggrieved by an order may obtain review of the order in the U.S. court of appeals for the circuit in which the violation allegedly occurred. Within 60 days of the issuance of the order, the petition for review must be filed and review shall conform to 5 U.S.C.§§ 701 *et seq.* An order of the Secretary shall not be subject to judicial review in any criminal or other civil proceeding. Whenever a person has failed to comply with an order, the Secretary will file a civil action in the U.S. district court for the district in which the violation occurred. In actions brought under the SDWA's whistleblower provisions, the district courts shall have jurisdiction to grant all appropriate relief, including injunctive relief and compensatory and exemplary damages.[36]

SARBANES-OXLEY ACT OF 2002 (SOX)

SOX prohibits publicly traded companies, including any subsidiaries or affiliates whose financial information is included in the consolidated financial statements of such companies, and nationally recognized statistical rating organizations from discharging, demoting, suspending, threatening, harassing, or in any other manner discriminating against an employee because such employee provided information, caused information to be provided, otherwise assisted in an investigation or filed, testified, or participated in a proceeding regarding any conduct that the employee reasonably believes is a violation of SOX, any SEC rule or regulation, or any federal statute relating to fraud against shareholders, when the information or assistance is provided to a federal regulatory or law enforcement agency, any Member or committee of Congress, or a person with supervisory authority over the employee or investigative authority for the employer, regarding any violation of 18 U.S.C. §§ 1341 (mail fraud), 1343 (wire fraud), 1344 (bank fraud), 1348 (securities fraud against shareholders), or any SEC rule or regulation, or of any federal law regarding fraud against shareholders.[37] Any employee who alleges such wrongful discharge or other discrimination may file a complaint with the Secretary of Labor, using procedures set forth in 49 U.S.C. § 42121(b). In the absence of delay resulting from an employee's bad faith, the employee may seek *de novo* review in the appropriate U.S. district court, if the Secretary of Labor does not issue a final decision within 180 days. An action must be commenced within 180 days after the date on which the violation occurs.[38]

A prevailing employee may be awarded all relief necessary to make the individual whole, including reinstatement with pre-discrimination seniority status, back pay with interest, and compensation for any special damages incurred as a result of the discrimination, including litigation costs, expert witness fees, and reasonable attorneys fees, and to leave the employee with all rights, privileges or remedies under federal or state law or any collective bargaining agreement.[39]

An employee prevailing in a whistleblower action may be awarded all relief necessary to make the individual whole.

SOLID WASTE DISPOSAL ACT (SWDA)

The SWDA prohibits employers from firing, or in any other way discriminating against, or causing to be fired or discriminated against, any employee because such employee filed, instituted, or caused to be filed or instituted any proceeding under the SWDA, or has testified or is about to testify in any proceeding resulting from the administration or enforcement of the SWDA.[40] Any employee who believes that he or she has been fired or otherwise discriminated against in violation of the SWDA's whistleblower provisions may, within 30 days after such alleged violation occurs, apply to the Secretary of Labor for a review. Upon receipt of such application, the Secretary will institute an investigation as she deems appropriate. Following the receipt of the investigation report, the Secretary will make findings of fact; if she finds that a violation did occur, the Secretary will issue a decision, incorporating an order and findings, requiring the party committing such violation to take such affirmative action to abate the violation, including the rehiring or reinstatement of the employee with compensation. If the Secretary finds no violation, she will issue an order denying the application; such order shall be subject to judicial review in the same manner as orders and decisions are subject to judicial review under 42 U.S.C. §§ 6901 et seq.[41] Whenever an order is issued, at the request of the applicant, a sum equal to the aggregate amount of all costs and expenses, including attorneys' fees, to have been reasonably incurred by the applicant, will be assessed against the person who committed the violation.[42]

SURFACE MINING CONTROL AND RECLAMATION ACT (SMCRA)

The SMCRA prohibits employers from discharging or in any other way discriminating against or causing to be fired or discriminated against any employee because such employee has filed, instituted, or caused to be filed or instituted any proceeding under this provision. Additionally, any employee who has testified or is about to testify in any such proceedings is protected from such retaliatory action.[43] An employee who believes that he or she has been fired or otherwise discriminated against in violation of the SMCRA's whistleblower provisions may, within 30 days, apply to the Secretary of Labor for a review of such firing or alleged discrimination. Upon receipt of such complaint, the Secretary will initiate an investigation as she deems appropriate. If the Secretary determines that a violation occurred, she will issue a decision incorporating the findings of fact and an order requiring the party committing the violation to take such affirmative action to abate the violation as the Secretary deems appropriate, including the rehiring or reinstatement of the employee with compensation. If the Secretary finds that no violation occurred, she shall issue a finding. Orders issued by the Secretary shall be subject to judicial review in the same manner as other orders and decisions of the Secretary are subject to judicial review under the SMCRA.[44] Whenever an order is issued to abate a violation, at the request of the applicant, a sum equal to the aggregate amount of all costs and expenses, including attorney's fees, determined to have been reasonably incurred by the applicant in connection with the institution and prosecution of such proceedings, shall be assessed against the person who committed the violation.[45]

TOXIC SUBSTANCES CONTROL ACT (TSCA)

The TSCA prohibits employers from discharging or otherwise discriminating against any employee with respect to compensation, terms, conditions, or privileges of employment because the employee has (1) commenced, caused to be commenced, or is about to commence or cause to be commenced a proceeding under the TSCA; (2) testified or is about to testify in any such proceeding; or (3) assisted or participated or is about to assist or participate in such a proceeding or in any other action to carry out the purposes of the TSCA.[46] Any employee who believes that he or she has been discharged or otherwise discriminated against by any person in violation of the TSCA's whistleblower provisions may, within 30 days after such alleged violation occurs, file a complaint with the Secretary of Labor. Upon receipt of such a complaint, the Secretary will conduct an investigation and within 30 days of the receipt of such complaint, the Secretary will complete such investigation. Within 90 days of receiving the complaint, the Secretary will, unless the proceeding is terminated due to a settlement, issue an order either providing relief or denying the complaint. The Secretary may not enter into a settlement terminating a proceeding on a complaint without the participation and consent of the complainant. If the Secretary determines that a violation of this provision has occurred, the Secretary will (1) order the person who committed such violation to take affirmative action to abate the violation, (2) order such person to reinstate the complainant to the complainant's former position together with the compensation, including backpay, terms, conditions, and privileges of the complainant's employment, (3) order compensatory damages, and (4) where appropriate, order exemplary damages. Whenever an order is issued, at the request of the applicant, a sum equal to the aggregate amount of all costs and expenses, including attorneys' fees will be assessed against the person who committed the violation.[47] Any employee or employer adversely affected or aggrieved by an order may obtain review of the order in the U.S. court of appeals for the circuit in which the violation allegedly occurred. The petition for review must be filed within 60 days of the issuance of the order. Such review must conform to 5 U.S.C.§§ 701 *et seq.* Whenever a person has failed to comply with an order, the Secretary will file a civil action in the U.S. district court for the district in which the violation was found to occur. In actions brought under the TSCA's whistleblower provisions, the district courts shall have jurisdiction to grant all appropriate relief, including injunctive relief and compensatory and exemplary damages.[48]

WHISTLEBLOWER PROTECTION ACT (WPA)

The WPA[49] generally provides protections for federal employees who make disclosures evidencing illegal or improper government activities. In order to trigger the protections of the WPA, a case must contain the following elements: a "personnel action" that was taken because of a "protected disclosure" made by a "covered employee."

Covered Employees

Although anyone may disclose whistleblowing information for referral to the appropriate agency, an investigation and report from the head of that agency is required only if the information is received from a "covered employee." In addition, with few exceptions, prohibited personnel practices apply only to covered employees. Therefore, as a threshold matter, it is important to note which federal employees are statutorily covered.

> To trigger protections under the WPA, a case must contain the following elements, as defined under the act:
>
> - A personnel action
> - A protected disclosure
> - A covered employee

Generally, current employees, former employees, or applicants for employment to positions in the executive branch of government and the Government Printing Office, in both the competitive and the excepted service, as well as positions in the Senior Executive Service, are considered covered employees.[50] However, those positions that are excepted from the competitive service because of their "confidential, policy-determining, policy-making, or policy-advocating character,"[51] and any positions exempted by the President based on a determination that it is necessary and warranted by conditions of good administration,[52] are not protected by the whistleblower statute.

Moreover, the statute does not apply to federal workers employed by the U.S. Postal Service or the Postal Rate Commission,[53] the Government Accountability Office, the Federal Bureau of Investigation,[54] the Central Intelligence Agency, the Defense Intelligence Agency, the National Geospatial-Intelligence Agency, the National Security Agency, and any other executive entity that the President determines primarily conducts foreign intelligence or counter-intelligence activities.[55] Agency heads are required to inform their employees of these protections.[56]

Protected Disclosures

Any disclosure of information that a covered employee reasonably believes evidences "a violation of any law, rule, or regulation" or evidences "gross mismanagement, a gross waste of funds, an abuse of authority, or a substantial and specific danger to public health or safety" is protected on the condition that the disclosure is not prohibited by law nor required to be kept secret by Executive Order in the interest of national defense or foreign affairs.[57] Moreover, any disclosure made to the Special Counsel or to the Inspector General of an agency or another employee designated by the head of the agency to receive such disclosures, which the employee reasonably believes evidences "a violation of any law, rule, or regulation," or evidences "gross mismanagement, a gross waste of funds, an abuse of authority, or a substantial and specific danger to public health or safety" is also protected.[58] In addition, the WPA expressly provides that the statute is not to be interpreted as "authoriz[ing] the withholding of information from the Congress or the taking of any personnel action against an employee who discloses information to the Congress."[59]

Personnel Actions

The WPA protects employees from reprisals in the form of an agency taking or failing to take a "personnel action." This encompasses a broad range of actions by an agency having a negative or adverse impact on the employee. The statute specifically defines the term "personnel action" to include 11 areas of agency activity:

> (i) an appointment; (ii) a promotion; (iii) an action under chapter 75 of this title or other disciplinary or corrective action; (iv) a detail, transfer, or reassignment; (v) a reinstatement; (vi) a restoration; (vii) a reemployment; (viii) a performance evaluation under chapter 43 of this title; (ix) a decision concerning pay, benefits, or awards, or concerning education or training if the education or training may reasonably be expected to lead to an appointment, promotion, performance evaluation, or other action described in this subparagraph; (x) a decision to order psychiatric testing or examination; and (xi) any other significant change in duties, responsibilities, or working conditions.[60]

The WPA also expressly protects employees from prohibited personnel practices taken because they engaged in activities that are often related to whistleblowing, including exercising any appeal, complaint, or grievance right granted by law, rule, or regulation, testifying for others or lawfully assisting others in any such appeal, complaint, or grievance right; cooperating with or disclosing information to an agency Inspector General or the Special Counsel; or for refusing to obey an order that would be in violation of law.[61]

Forums Where Whistleblower Protections May Be Raised

Under the WPA, there are three general forums or proceedings where whistleblower protections may be raised: (A) in employee appeals to the Merit Systems Protection Board (MSPB) of an agency's adverse action against the employee under chapter 77;[62] (B) in actions instituted by the Office of Special Counsel (OSC);[63] and (C) in individual rights of action.[64] Beyond the statutory provisions of the WPA, the defense or claim of reprisal for whistleblowing might also be raised in a grievance proceeding initiated by an employee pursuant to a grievance procedure that was negotiated through collective bargaining between the employee's agency and the employee union.[65] An aggrieved employee affected by a prohibited personnel action is precluded from choosing more than one of the above remedies.[66]

Under the WPA, whistleblower protections may be raised in three general forums or proceedings:

1. Employee appeals to the MSPB under chapter 77
2. Actions instituted by the Office of Special Counsel
3. Individual rights of action

Employee Appeals to the MSPB under Chapter 77

The MSPB is authorized to hear and rule on appeals by employees regarding agency actions affecting the employee and that are appealable to the Board by law, rule, or regulation.[67] Types of agency actions against employees that are appealable to the MSPB and in which an employee may raise the defense of reprisal for whistleblowing as a prohibited personnel practice include adverse actions against the employee for "such cause as will promote the efficiency of the service" (generally referred to as conduct-based adverse actions),[68] and performance-based adverse actions against employees for "unacceptable performance."[69] In such appeals, an agency's decision and action will not be upheld if the employee "shows that the decision was based on any prohibited personnel practice described in section 2302(b) of this title."[70] If the MSPB finds that an employee or applicant for employment has prevailed in an appeal, the employee or applicant may be provided with interim relief, pending the outcome of any petition of review.[71] Moreover, the Special Counsel may not intervene in an appeal under chapter 77 without the consent of the individual bringing the appeal.[72]

Actions by the Office of Special Counsel (OSC)

The WPA established the OSC as an agency independent from the MSPB.[73] Its primary responsibilities, however, have remained essentially the same as set forth in its statutory predecessor, the Civil Service Reform Act (CSRA). With the goal of protecting employees, former employees, and applicants for employment from prohibited personnel practices, the OSC has the duty to receive allegations of prohibited personnel practices and to investigate such allegations,[74] as well as to conduct an investigation of possible prohibited personnel practices on its own initiative, absent any allegation.[75]

The Special Counsel has several avenues available through which to pursue allegations, complaints, and evidences of reprisals for whistleblowing activities, including (1) requiring agency investigations and agency reports concerning actions the agency is planning to take to rectify those matters referred;[76] (2) seeking an order for "corrective action" by the agency before the MSPB;[77] (3) seeking "disciplinary action" against officers and employees who have committed prohibited personnel practices;[78] (4) intervening in any proceedings before the MSPB, except that in cases where an individual has brought an individual right of action (IRA) under Section 1221 or an appeal to the MSPB under chapter 77, the OSC must first obtain the individual's consent;[79] and (5) seeking a stay from the MSPB for any personnel action pending an investigation.[80]

Investigations[81]

Within 240 days of receipt of a complaint, the OSC must make a determination as to whether there are reasonable grounds to believe that a prohibited personnel practice has occurred, exists, or is to be taken.[82] If a positive determination is made and the information was sent to the Special Counsel by an employee, former employee, applicant for employment, or an employee who obtained the information acting within the scope of employment,[83] the Special Counsel must transmit the information to the appropriate agency head and require that the agency head conduct an investigation and submit a written report.[84] The identity of the complaining employee may not be disclosed without such individual's consent, unless the Special Counsel determines that disclosure is necessary to avoid imminent danger to health and safety or an imminent criminal violation.[85] The Special Counsel then reviews the reports as to their completeness and the reasonableness of the findings[86] and submits the reports to Congress, the President, the Comptroller General,[87] and the complainant.[88]

If the Special Counsel does not make a positive determination, however, he or she may only transmit the information to the agency head with the consent of the individual.[89] Further, if the Special Counsel receives the information from some source other than the ones described above, he or she *may* transmit the information to the appropriate agency head who shall inform the Special Counsel of any action taken.[90] In any case where the subject of the whistleblowing disclosure evidences a criminal violation, however, all information is referred to the Attorney General and no report is transmitted to the complainant.[91]

At least every 60 days throughout its investigation, the OSC must give notice of the status of the investigation to the individual who brought the allegation.[92] In addition, no later than 10 days before the termination of an investigation, a written status report including the proposed findings and legal conclusions must be made to the individual who made the allegation of wrongdoing.[93]

Corrective Actions

If in any investigation the Special Counsel determines that there are "reasonable grounds to believe" a prohibited personnel practice exists or has occurred, the Special Counsel must report findings and recommendations, and may include recommendations for corrective action, to the MSPB, the agency involved, the Office of Personnel Management (OPM) and, optionally, to the President.[94] If the agency does not act to correct the prohibited personnel practice, the Special Counsel may petition the MSPB for corrective action.[95] The MSPB, before rendering its decision, is required to provide an opportunity for oral or written comments by the Special Counsel, the agency involved and the OPM, and for written comments by any individual who alleges to be the victim of the prohibited personnel practices.[96]

The WPA made it easier for a complainant to prove retaliation for whistleblowing in a corrective action before the MSPB. The Special Counsel need only prove by a preponderance of the evidence that the disclosure was a "contributing factor" in the personnel action, instead of a "significant factor."[97] In addition, once the MSPB renders a final order or decision of corrective action, complainants have the right to judicial review in the U.S. Court of Appeals for the Federal Circuit.[98]

In what is probably the most significant change from its statutory predecessor, the CSRA, the WPA increased the standard by which an agency must prove its affirmative defense that it would have taken the personnel action even if the employee had not engaged in protected conduct. Once the complainant's *prima facie* case of reprisal has been established by showing that the whistleblowing was a contributing factor in the personnel action, the government is required to demonstrate by "clear and convincing evidence" that it would have taken the same personnel action even in the absence of such disclosure.[99] Under the CSRA, the government's standard of proof was a "preponderance of the evidence." "Clear and convincing evidence," although a lesser standard than the criminal standard of "beyond a reasonable doubt," is greater than "preponderance of the evidence."

Disciplinary Actions

Proceedings for disciplinary action against an officer or employee who commits a prohibited personnel practice may be instituted by the Special Counsel by filing a written complaint with the MSPB.[100] After proceedings before the MSPB or an administrative law judge,[101] if violations are found, the MSPB may impose any of various disciplinary actions, including removal, reduction in grade, debarment from federal employment for a period not to exceed five years, suspension, reprimand, or an assessment of civil fines up to $1,000.[102] In addition, the agency involved may be held responsible for reasonable attorney's fees.[103] In the case of presidentially appointed and Senate confirmed employees in "confidential, policy-making, policy-determining, or policy-advocating" positions, the complaint and the statement of facts, along with any response from the employee, are to be presented to the President for disposition in lieu of the presentation to the Board.[104]

Intervention

As a matter of right, the Special Counsel may intervene or otherwise participate in any proceedings before the MSPB, except that in cases where an individual has brought an individual right of action (IRA) under Section 1221, discussed below, or an appeal to the MSPB under chapter 77, the OSC must first obtain the individual's consent.[105]

Stays

Upon application by the OSC, a member of the MSPB may stay or postpone, for 45 days, pending an investigation, a personnel action that the Special Counsel has reasonable grounds to believe constitutes a prohibited personnel practice, unless the member determines that a stay would not be appropriate under the circumstances.[106] If no MSPB member acts within three days of the OSC application, the stay becomes effective.[107] After the employing agency has had an opportunity to comment on the appropriateness of extending a stay, the MSPB may extend it.[108] A stay may be terminated by the MSPB at any time, except that a stay may not be terminated by the MSPB on its own motion or on the motion of an agency, unless notice and opportunity for oral or written comments are first provided to the Special Counsel and the individual on whose behalf the stay was ordered; or on a motion of the Special Counsel, unless notice and opportunity for oral or written comments are first provided to the individual on whose behalf the stay was ordered.[109]

Individual Right of Action (IRA)

The WPA provides that an employee, former employee, or applicant for employment has the independent right to seek review of whistleblower reprisal cases by the MSPB no more than 60 days after notification is provided to such employee that the investigation was closed or 120 days after filing a complaint with the OSC.[110] As a result of the IRA statutory provisions, a greater number of employees, including probationers, temporaries, and those in the excepted service, have a method of appeal to the MSPB for whistleblower reprisals that was not previously available under the CSRA.[111] In addition, retired employees are not barred from instituting this type of appeal.[112]

If the employee is the prevailing party before the MSPB, based on the finding of a prohibited personnel practice, or if the employee is the prevailing party in an appeal to the MSPB, regardless of the basis of the decision, the WPA provides several remedies. These may include placing the individual, as nearly as possible, in the position the individual would have been in had the prohibited personnel practice not occurred, awarding back pay and related benefits, recompensing medical costs incurred, travel expenses, or any other reasonable and foreseeable consequential charges.[113] In all cases, corrective action includes awarding attorneys' fees.[114] The MSPB findings can be based on circumstantial evidence.[115] Moreover, the Special Counsel may not intervene in an individual right of action without the consent of the individual bringing the appeal.[116]

End Notes

[1] P.L. 111-353, 124 Stat. 3885.
[2] 42 U.S.C. § 7622(a).
[3] 42 U.S.C. § 7622(b).
[4] 42 U.S.C. § 7622(d).
[5] 42 U.S.C. § 7622(e).

[6] 49 U.S.C. § 31105(a).
[7] 49 U.S.C. § 31105(b).
[8] 49 U.S.C. § 31105(c), (d).
[9] 42 U.S.C. § 9610(a).
[10] 42 U.S.C. § 9610(b).
[11] 42 U.S.C. § 9610(c).
[12] 10 U.S.C. § 2409(a).
[13] 10 U.S.C. § 2409(b).
[14] 10 U.S.C. § 2409(c)(1).
[15] 10 U.S.C. § 2409(c)(2).
[16] 10 U.S.C. § 2409(c)(3).
[17] See P.L. 111-203, § 748, 124 Stat. 1376, 1739 (2010).
[18] P.L. 111-203, § 1057(a), 124 Stat. 1376, 2031 (2010). The term "covered employee" is defined to include "any individual performing tasks related to the offering or provision of a consumer financial product or service."
[19] P.L. 111-203, § 1057(c)(2)(C), 124 Stat. 1376, 2032-33 (2010).
[20] 42 U.S.C. § 5851(b).
[21] Id.
[22] 42 U.S.C. § 5851(c).
[23] 29 U.S.C. § 215(a)(3).
[24] 29 U.S.C. § 216(b).
[25] 21 U.S.C. § 1012(a).
[26] 21 U.S.C. § 1012(b)(1).
[27] 30 U.S.C. § 815(c)(1).
[28] 30 U.S.C. § 815(c)(2).
[29] 30 U.S.C. § 816.
[30] 33 U.S.C. § 1367(a).
[31] 33 U.S.C. § 948a.
[32] 29 U.S.C. § 1855(a).
[33] 29 U.S.C. § 1855(b).
[34] 29 U.S.C. § 660(c).
[35] 42 U.S.C. § 300j-9(i)(1),(2).
[36] 42 U.S.C. § 300j-9(i)(3),(4).
[37] 18 U.S.C. § 1514A(a).
[38] 18 U.S.C. § 1514A(b)(2)(D).
[39] 18 U.S.C. § 1514A(c), (d).
[40] 42 U.S.C. § 6971(a).
[41] 42 U.S.C. § 6971(b).
[42] 42 U.S.C. § 6971(c).
[43] 30 U.S.C. § 1293(a).
[44] 30 U.S.C. § 1293(b).
[45] 30 U.S.C. §1293(c).
[46] 15 U.S.C. § 2622(a).
[47] 15 U.S.C. § 2622(b).
[48] 15 U.S.C. § 2622(c),(d).
[49] P.L. 101-12, 103 Stat. 16; P.L. 103-424, 108 Stat. 4361 (codified, as amended, in various sections of Title 5 U.S.C.).
[50] 5 U.S.C. § 2302(a)(2)(B).

[51] 5 U.S.C. § 2302(a)(2)(B)(i).

[52] 5 U.S.C. § 2302(a)(2)(B)(ii).

[53] 5 U.S.C. § 2105(e).

[54] Another provision of federal law prohibits personnel practices in the FBI as a reprisal for a disclosure of information to the Attorney General or his or her designee that the employee reasonably believes evidences "(1) a violation of any law, rule, or regulation, or (2) mismanagement, a gross waste of funds, an abuse of authority, or a substantial and specific danger to public health or safety." 5 U.S.C. § 2303(a)(1),(2).

[55] 5 U.S.C. § 2302(a)(2)(C).

[56] 5 U.S.C. § 2302(c).

[57] 5 U.S.C. § 2302(b)(8)(A).

[58] 5 U.S.C. § 2302(b)(8)(B).

[59] 5 U.S.C. § 2302(b). Based on the legislative history regarding this provision of the WPA, it appears that Congress sought to protect its right to receive even "confidential" information from federal employees, without employee fear of reprisals: The provision is intended to make clear that by placing limitations on the kinds of information any employee may publicly disclose without suffering reprisal, there is not intent to limit the information an employee may provide to Congress or to authorize reprisal against an employee for providing information to Congress. For example, 18 U.S.C. 1905 prohibits public disclosure of information involving trade secrets. That statute does not apply to transmittal of such information by an agency to Congress. Section 2302(b)(8) of this act would not protect an employee against reprisal for public disclosure of such statutorily protected information, but it is not to be inferred that an employee is similarly un-protected if such disclosure is made to the appropriate unit of the Congress. Neither title I nor any other provision of the act should be construed as limiting in any way the rights of employees to communicate with or testify before Congress. H.Rept. 95-1717 (Conference Report) (1978), reprinted in 1978 U.S. CODE CONG. & ADMIN. NEWS 2861. See also 5 U.S.C. § 7211, providing that an employee is guaranteed the right to freely petition or furnish information to Congress, a Member of Congress, a committee, or a Member thereof.

[60] 5 U.S.C. § 2302(a)(2)(A).

[61] 5 U.S.C. § 2302(b)(9).

[62] 5 U.S.C. § 7701.

[63] 5 U.S.C. §§ 1211-1215.

[64] 5 U.S.C. § 1221.

[65] 5 U.S.C. § 7121.

[66] 5 U.S.C. § 7121(g)(2).

[67] 5 U.S.C. § 7701, 5 U.S.C. § 1205.

[68] 5 U.S.C. § 7513(a).

[69] 5 U.S.C. § 4303(a).

[70] 5 U.S.C. § 7701(c)(2)(B).

[71] 5 U.S.C. § 7701(b)(2)(A).

[72] 5 U.S.C. § 1212(c)(2).

[73] 5 U.S.C. § 1211(a). It provides that the Office of Special Counsel (OSC) will be headed by the Special Counsel and have a judicially noted official seal. The Senate report states that although the MSPB and the OSC had "separated themselves administratively in 1984," the whistleblower legislation "completes this process by establishing the OSC as an independent agency." S.Rept. 100-413 at 18. Moreover, the statute provides that the Special Counsel, appointed by the President, with the advice and consent of the Senate, may only be

removed from office for "inefficiency, neglect of duty, or malfeasance in office." 5 U.S.C. § 1211(b).

[74] 5 U.S.C. § 1212(a)(2).

[75] 5 U.S.C. § 1214(a)(5).

[76] 5 U.S.C. § 1213(c).

[77] 5 U.S.C. § 1214(b)(2).

[78] 5 U.S.C. § 1215(b).

[79] 5 U.S.C. § 1212(c).

[80] 5 U.S.C. § 1212(b)(1).

[81] In addition to investigating whether prohibited personnel actions have been taken because of protected whistleblowing disclosures, the WPA also charges the OSC with investigating whether there is a "substantial likelihood" that whistleblowing disclosures evidence violations of a law, rule or regulation. 5 U.S.C. §1213(b).

[82] 5 U.S.C. § 1214(b)(2)(A)(i).

[83] 5 U.S.C. § 1213(c)(2).

[84] 5 U.S.C. § 1213(c)(1).

[85] 5 U.S.C. § 1213(h).

[86] 5 U.S.C. § 1213(e)(2).

[87] 5 U.S.C. § 1213(e)(3).

[88] 5 U.S.C. § 1213(e)(1).

[89] 5 U.S.C. § 1213(g)(2).

[90] 5 U.S.C. § 1213(g)(1).

[91] 5 U.S.C. § 1213(f).

[92] 5 U.S.C. § 1214(a)(1)(C)(ii).

[93] 5 U.S.C. § 1214(a)(1)(D).

[94] 5 U.S.C. § 1214(b)(2)(B).

[95] 5 U.S.C. § 1214(b)(2)(C).

[96] 5 U.S.C. § 1214(b)(3).

[97] 5 U.S.C. §1214(b)(4)(i).

[98] 5 U.S.C. § 1214(c).

[99] 5 U.S.C. § 1214(b)(4)(B).

[100] 5 U.S.C. § 1215(a)(1).

[101] 5 U.S.C. § 1215(a)(2)(C).

[102] 5 U.S.C. § 1215(a)(3).

[103] 5 U.S.C. § 1204(m)(1).

[104] 5 U.S.C. § 1215(b).

[105] 5 U.S.C. § 1212(c).

[106] 5 U.S.C. § 1214(b)(1)(A)(i),(ii).

[107] 5 U.S.C. § 1214(b)(1)(A)(iii).

[108] 5 U.S.C. § 1214(b)(1)(B),(C).

[109] 5 U.S.C. § 1214(b)(1)(D).

[110] 5 U.S.C. §§ 1221, 1214(a)(3).

[111] 5 U.S.C. § 7701.

[112] 5 U.S.C. § 1221(j).

[113] 5 U.S.C. § 1221(g)(1)(A)(i),(ii).

[114] 5 U.S.C. § 1221(g)(1)(B).

[115] 5 U.S.C. § 1221(e)(1).

[116] 5 U.S.C. § 1212(c)(2).

In: Whistleblowers:
Editor: Andre Pope
ISBN: 978-1-63482-290-9

Chapter 3

WHISTLEBLOWER PROTECTION PROGRAM: OPPORTUNITIES EXIST FOR OSHA AND DOT TO STRENGTHEN COLLABORATIVE MECHANISMS*

United States Government Accountability Office

ABBREVIATIONS

ALJ	Administrative Law Judge
AIR21	Wendell H. Ford Aviation Investment and Reform Act of the 21st Century
ARB	Administrative Review Board
DOT	Department of Transportation
FAA	Federal Aviation Administration
FMCSA	Federal Motor Carrier Safety Administration
FRA	Federal Railroad Administration
FRSA	Federal Railroad Safety Act
FTA	Federal Transit Administration
MAP-21	Moving Ahead for Progress in the 21st Century Act
MOA	memorandums of agreement

* This is an edited, reformatted and augmented version of The United States Government Accountability Office publication, GAO-14-286, Report to Congressional Requesters, dated March 2014.

NHTSA	National Highway Traffic Safety Administration
NTSSA	National Transit Systems Security Act
PHMSA	Pipeline and Hazardous Materials Safety Administration
PSIA	Pipeline Safety Improvement Act
OALJ	Office of Administrative Law Judges
OSHA	Occupational Safety and Health Administration
STAA	Surface Transportation Assistance Act

Why GAO Did This Study

Transportation workers who "blow the whistle" on prohibited practices can help ensure that their employers comply with federal laws. Within the Department of Labor, OSHA investigates whistleblower claims, filed by transportation employees who believe their employers have retaliated against them for reporting unlawful practices. The Moving Ahead for Progress in the 21st Century Act (MAP-21), required OSHA to establish protections for auto industry employees and required GAO to review OSHA's efforts and transportation-related whistleblower claims. GAO examined (1) steps OSHA has taken to include auto industry employees in its whistleblower program and the extent to which OSHA collaborated with DOT components to address potential safety violations, and (2) the number of transportation-related whistleblower claims in the last 6 years and stakeholder-identified factors that may affect those numbers. GAO compared agency documents against key practices for collaboration, and interviewed federal agency officials and stakeholders representing transportation modes covered by these statutes to identify factors that may affect the number of whistleblower claims reported by OSHA.

What GAO Recommends

OSHA and DOT should evaluate their current and in-process MOAs and incorporate key practices for collaboration. Neither agency agreed or disagreed with the recommendation. OSHA stated that it believes its MOAs incorporate key practices, but GAO continues to believe the MOAs can be strengthened.

WHAT GAO FOUND

The Occupational Safety and Health Administration (OSHA) has taken steps to include auto industry employees in its Whistleblower Protection Program and has coordinated with the Department of Transportation (DOT) on whistleblower issues, but interagency collaborative mechanisms could be strengthened. Among other steps, OSHA is developing procedures for how it will investigate claims from auto employees and estimates most of its efforts will be completed in 2014. OSHA documents its collaboration with DOT's component agencies on whistleblower protections by developing memorandums of agreements (MOA), and currently MOAs cover aviation and rail employees; the agencies are considering developing MOAs to cover other transportation sectors such as commercial motor-carrier employees. Officials from both OSHA and DOT believe it is important to identify or refer potential claims of retaliation and safety violations to each other. In September 2012, GAO concluded that collaboration is critical when meaningful results that the federal government seeks to achieve require the coordinated efforts of more than one federal agency. Among others, key practices of effective collaboration include clearly delineating roles and responsibilities and monitoring progress. OSHA and DOT officials agree that following GAO's key practices would be beneficial. However, the agencies have an opportunity to strengthen current and future MOAs by clearly delineating roles and responsibilities, and determining how the agencies' efforts will be monitored and evaluated. For example, the current MOAs do not clearly define agency roles and responsibilities with respect to developing training on whistleblower issues and regional coordination. Defining such responsibilities could help ensure beneficial training occurs and the agencies avoid miscommunication and inconsistent whistleblower processes involving referrals between the agencies' regional offices. Additionally, since the agencies have not developed or documented how they would monitor referrals, neither OSHA nor DOT can assess whether the referral process is working as intended. By monitoring and evaluating the outcomes of referrals, the agencies would have more assurance that they are addressing the safety violations and claims of retaliation raised by transportation-related employees.

The number of transportation-related whistleblower claims filed with OSHA has increased in the last 6 years—from 508 in fiscal year 2008 to 821 in fiscal year 2013—and GAO's interviews with transportation industry stakeholders identified several factors that might affect those numbers and how they could be interpreted. These factors include multiple avenues to address safety issues, employee awareness of whistleblower protections, and statutory whistleblower provisions, among others. The identified factors are not mutually exclusive and could either increase or decrease the number of whistleblower claims. For example, officials representing three transportation modes noted that multiple safety-reporting mechanisms, such as anonymous hotlines, can indirectly affect whether employees file whistleblower claims since employees are less likely to face retaliation when reporting safety issues anonymously. Regarding statutory whistleblower provisions, the statute covering rail employees provides the largest number of protected activities, and this protection, according to rail industry officials, has enabled rail employees to file more whistleblower claims than other transportation employees.

* * *

March 19, 2014

The Honorable John D. Rockefeller IV
Chairman

The Honorable John Thune
Ranking Member
Committee on Commerce, Science, and Transportation
United States Senate

The Honorable Fred Upton
Chairman

The Honorable Henry A. Waxman
Ranking Member
Committee on Energy and Commerce
House of Representatives

Transportation industry employees who "blow the whistle" on prohibited or unlawful practices they discover through their employment can play an important role in ensuring that their employers comply with federal laws. Currently, there are six federal statutes that prohibit employers in various transportation industries from discriminating or retaliating against these employees.[1] If whistleblowers in these transportation industries believe they experienced reprisals (such as being fired) for participating in protected activities, they can file a claim with the Department of Labor's Occupational Safety and Health Administration (OSHA). Through its Whistleblower Protection Program, OSHA investigates and reviews whistleblower claims.[2] To carry out its responsibilities for investigating whistleblower claims, OSHA coordinates with relevant federal agencies that oversee those industries. For example, in the case of the various transportation-related statutes, OSHA coordinates with the Department of Transportation (DOT). As the federal agency responsible for developing and enforcing regulations to ensure a safe transportation system that employers in the transportation sectors must follow, DOT investigates potential transportation-related safety issues to determine whether any DOT regulations have been violated.

The Moving Ahead for Progress in the 21st Century Act (MAP-21), enacted in 2012, mandated protections for individuals employed in the auto industry and expanded OSHA's responsibility to investigate the whistleblower claims from auto industry workers.[3] MAP-21 also directed that we review OSHA's efforts to include auto industry workers in the Whistleblower Protection Program.[4] In this report, we present information on (1) the steps OSHA has taken to include auto industry employees in its DOT whistleblower program and the extent to which OSHA has collaborated with DOT components to address potential safety violations, and (2) the number of transportation-related whistleblower claims in the last 6 years and stakeholder-identified factors that might affect those numbers. We also present information on the differences in the transportation-related whistleblower statutes (see app. I) and the disposition of claims.

To address these issues, we examined the whistleblower provisions of the six statutes covering transportation workers in industries regulated by[5]: (1) MAP-21,[6] (2) the Federal Railroad Safety Act,[7] (3) the National Transit Systems Security Act,[8] (4) the Surface Transportation Assistance Act,[9] (5) the Pipeline Safety Improvement Act,[10] and (6) the Wendell H. Ford Aviation Investment and Reform Act for 21st Century.[11] We reviewed our previous reports on whistleblower protections and pertinent documentation from OSHA and DOT, including memorandums of agreement (MOA), and interviewed key federal agency officials on efforts to coordinate whistleblower protections for employees in the transportation industry. We compared the agencies' MOAs with our key practices for effective collaboration.[12] We also analyzed OSHA data on the number of whistleblower claims for fiscal years 2008 to 2013 and the disposition of claims in fiscal year 2013. To determine the reliability of OSHA's data on whistleblower claims, we reviewed relevant documentation and interviewed cognizant officials about their processes for reviewing the data and ensuring their accuracy. We determined the data used to be sufficiently reliable with attribution to official sources for conveying general information on OSHA's receipt of complaints over the last 6 years and claim dispositions for fiscal year 2013.

To identify factors affecting whistleblower claims, we interviewed a broad array of stakeholders from 44 organizations representing six different transportation industries. The stakeholders include officials from organizations representing employees and employers in the different transportation industries and nonprofit and advocacy groups representing whistleblowers. We selected these stakeholders because among other things, they are significant stakeholders in the transportation industries, and they represented a significant number of members in each of the six transportation industries; they were also referred by other stakeholders, including federal government officials and experts in whistleblower issues. The factors we identified are based on information gathered from the stakeholders and should not be viewed as identifying all factors that could affect the number of whistleblower claims made; however, the factors were consistently raised by the various stakeholders. The factors we report are limited to those identified by the stakeholders noted above and may not include all factors that could be identified. Also, the factors that we have identified should not be viewed as being representative of all transportation sector representatives and stakeholders.

We conducted this performance audit from May 2013 to March 2014 in accordance with generally accepted government auditing standards. Those standards require that we plan and perform the audit to obtain sufficient, appropriate evidence to provide a reasonable basis for our findings and conclusions based on our audit objectives. We believe that the evidence obtained provides a reasonable basis for our findings and conclusions based on our audit objectives. Further details on our scope and methodology can be found in appendix II.

BACKGROUND

As the primary federal agency responsible for administering the Whistleblower Protection Program, OSHA is responsible for investigating whistleblower claims under 22 statutes, 6 of which contain protections for employees in the transportation industries who are regulated by DOT. The 6 transportation-related statutes also include basic transportation safety provisions, which are administered by different DOT component agencies, as shown in figure 1. While OSHA investigates whistleblower claims, DOT investigates potential safety violations to determine whether any of its regulations have been violated and can refer employees alleging retaliation to OSHA. In fiscal year 2012, OSHA had a budget of approximately $16 million and 119 full-time employees to administer the whistleblower program.

Transportation-related statutes	Year of enactment of whistleblower provision	Employees covered	DOT component administering transportation safety provision	Approximate number of employees in industry in 2012 (in thousands)
Federal Railroad Safety Act (FRSA)	1980[a]	Employees of railroad carriers, or contractors or subcontractors	Federal Railroad Administration (FRA) and Federal Transit Administration (FTA)	287
Surface Transportation Assistance Act (STAA)	1983	Private sector drivers, including independent contractors while personally operating a commercial motor vehicle and other employees of commercial motor carriers	Federal Motor Carrier Safety Administration (FMCSA)	2,263
Wendell H. Ford Aviation Investment and Reform Act (AIR21)	2000	Employees of air carriers or their contractors or subcontractors. Contractors are defined as companies that perform safety sensitive functions by contract for air carriers	Federal Aviation Administration (FAA)	1,117
Pipeline Safety Improvement Act (PSIA)	2002	Employees of pipeline facilities, contractors or subcontractors	Pipeline and Hazardous Materials Safety Administration (PHMSA)	172
National Transit Systems Security Act (NTSSA)	2007	Employees of public transportation agencies or their contractors or subcontractors, if the public transportation agencies provide regular and continuing general or special transportation to the public (e.g., subway, commuter rail, bus system)	Federal Transit Administration (FTA)	373
Moving Ahead for Progress in the 21st Century Act (MAP-21)	2012	Employees of motor vehicle manufacturers, part suppliers, and dealerships	National Highway Traffic Safety Administration (NHTSA)	3,709

Source: GAO analysis of transportation-related statutes, OSHA data and Bureau of Labor Statistics Current Employment Survey.

[a] FRSA was amended in 2007 to assign responsibility for the whistleblower protections to the Department of Labor.

Figure 1. Information on Department of Transportation Whistleblower Statutes.

As shown in figure 2, there are several steps in the OSHA whistleblower claims process that employees in transportation-related industries follow.

- First, transportation industry employees file retaliation complaints with OSHA. A complaint should address the *prima facie* elements of a violation—that is, the complainant should state that the employee engaged in protected activity, the employer knew about the protected activity, the employer subjected the employee to an adverse action (such as being fired or demoted), and the protected activity contributed to the adverse action. OSHA investigators will screen a whistleblower claim for these prima facie elements and, if not met, dismiss the claim.

Source: GAO and OSHA.

Figure 2. Federal Whistleblower Investigation and Review Process.

- Second, for claims meeting the prima facie standard, OSHA's regional offices conduct an investigation. OSHA's whistleblower investigation process involves the following key steps: receive and screen complaint, investigate the claim, and write final report and notify the parties. If OSHA's investigation shows the complaint does not have merit (no reasonable cause to believe there was retaliation), the claim is dismissed. If the investigation leads to the Secretary of Labor's finding of merit (reasonable cause to believe there was retaliation), OSHA issues its finding and a preliminary order, which generally includes reinstatement to the employee's previous position and back pay and may order other monetary relief. If neither party files an objection within the required time frames, the findings and the preliminary order become final. (See app. I for information on each statute's time frames.)
- Third, if either party objects to the Secretary's findings or preliminary order, under the DOT transportation-related statutes, either party may request a hearing before one of the Department of Labor's Administrative Law Judges (ALJ). This review is *de novo*—it does not take into account the Secretary's findings from the OSHA investigation. The ALJ then makes a ruling that either upholds or overturns the Secretary's finding.
- Fourth, if either party objects to the ALJ's decision, either party may petition for review of the ALJ's decision to the Administrative Review Board (ARB) which generally issues the Secretary of Labor's final decision.

- Fifth, ARB's final decision may be appealed to the appropriate federal court of appeal. Also, under some of the DOT transportation-related statutes, whistleblowers may file their complaint in federal district court if the Secretary of Labor does not issue a final decision within 210 days. See our prior work for detailed information on OSHA's whistleblower investigation process.[13]

The whistleblower protection process is generally prescribed in the six DOT transportation-related whistleblower statutes, which are supplemented by regulations that clarify and set forth specific requirements for the whistleblower protection process.[14] The statutes also provide some time-frames for filing whistleblower complaints, investigating whistleblower claims, and issuing a final decision. For instance, a whistleblower in the covered transportation industries generally has 180 days from when the retaliatory action took place to file a claim (except under AIR21, which requires claims to be made in 90 days). Once a claim has been filed, OSHA has 60 days to issue findings and in cases where there is reasonable cause to believe there was retaliation, a preliminary order. However, the process could take longer than the 60 days. (See app. I for more information on the differences in the statutory provisions.) Given these timeframes, in some cases, whistleblower claims can take years to move through the process, from initially filing the claim to completion of the appeals process.

OSHA has been challenged in its ability to conduct investigations in a timely manner. In 2009, we examined the processing times for whistleblower claims and challenges OSHA faced in administering the program.[15] At that time, OSHA faced two key challenges—it lacked a mechanism to adequately ensure the quality and consistency of investigations and many investigators reported they lacked resources, such as training, to do their jobs. We made recommendations intended to improve the Whistleblower Protection Program and enhance oversight; the Department of Labor took actions to address most of our recommendations, including revising its information database and providing training.[16]

OSHA Has Initiated Efforts to Include Auto Employees in Its Whistleblower Program, but Has Opportunities to Enhance Collaborative Mechanisms with DOT

OSHA Has Taken Preliminary Steps to Establish Whistleblower Protections for Auto Employees

OSHA is establishing whistleblower protections for auto industry employees as required under MAP-21. Specifically, OSHA has started to develop an interim final rule, investigative policies and procedures, and a fact sheet as follows:[17]

- *Interim final rule.* According to OSHA officials, the agency is in the early stages of developing an "interim final rule"[18] that will cover whistleblower claims filed under MAP-21. MAP-21's whistleblower provisions protect auto industry employees from retaliation by motor vehicle manufacturers, parts suppliers, and dealerships, for engaging in protected activity related to motor vehicle defects. The rule would, among other things, summarize the statutory whistleblower provisions and the available remedies, explain how to file a claim, and describe OSHA's investigative process. The rule was placed on the Department of Labor's fall 2013 regulatory agenda;[19] according to OSHA, the interim final rule is scheduled for publication in October 2014. At the time of our review, additional steps that OSHA planned to take in developing the rule included researching key issues, drafting the rule in consultation with the Solicitor of Labor, sharing the draft with the National Highway Traffic Safety Administration (NHTSA), obtaining agency and departmental clearance, and submitting the rule to Office of Management and Budget for review. OSHA officials told us they did not have a project plan or timeline for completing these tasks related to development of the rule, but OSHA did have a due date for the overall development of the interim final rule. The interim final rule will be effective once it is published (currently scheduled for October 2014) and there will be a 60-day public comment period. After the comment period, OSHA plans to review the public's comments and begin drafting a final rule, whereby the drafting and clearance steps described above are to be repeated. OSHA then plans to issue the final rule, which may incorporate changes based on comments the agency received.

- *Investigative policies and procedures.* OSHA is developing the policies and procedures for its investigators to use when reviewing claims filed by auto industry employees. According to OSHA, these policies and procedures will outline the procedures for handling retaliation complaints under the auto whistleblower statute and will be included in OSHA's Whistleblower Investigations Manual.[20] Until these procedures are finalized in fiscal year 2014, OSHA has instructed its investigators to follow procedures under the Consumer Product Safety Improvement Act of 2008, because the procedures under this statute are similar to the MAP-21 whistleblower statute for auto industry employees.[21]
- *Fact sheet.* OSHA is developing a whistleblower fact sheet that describes employees' protected activities under MAP-21 and how to report a claim of retaliation to OSHA. OSHA plans to publish the fact sheet for auto industry employees in 2014 and post it on its Whistleblower Protection Program webpage.[22]

OSHA and DOT Could Strengthen Their Collaborative Mechanisms

According to OSHA and DOT officials, memorandums of agreement (MOA) are key documents through which the agencies document their collaboration. Although MOAs are not required by law, officials at both agencies said that the MOAs provide benefits, such as establishing a process between the agencies to communicate, exchange information, and work on common issues involving transportation safety violations that may arise from whistleblower complaints. In addition, agency officials said the MOAs provide continuity between the agencies as agency staff change and help to ensure that current staff understand what information should be shared. The MOAs include, among other things, background information on the agencies' responsibilities and areas of cooperation.

OSHA has established MOAs or has plans under way to do so with several DOT components. For example, OSHA has established an MOA with the Federal Aviation Administration (FAA) covering aviation employees, and with the Federal Railroad Administration (FRA) covering rail employees in 2002 and 2012, respectively.[23] These MOAs are available on OSHA's website and transportation industry employees and the public can access the documents. Although OSHA had not yet established MOAs with DOT components covering the remaining transportation industries, OSHA officials told us they were in the process of developing an MOA with the Federal Motor Carrier Safety Administration (FMCSA) to cover commercial drivers and other motor carrier employees and the Pipeline and Hazardous Materials Safety Administration (PHMSA) to cover pipeline employees. OSHA officials said they plan to finalize the MOAs with FMCSA and PHMSA in 2014.[24] OSHA requested an introductory meeting with the Federal Transit Administration (FTA) to discuss whether an MOA is needed to cover public transit employees.[25] OSHA and NHTSA agreed that due to the low complaint volume under MAP-21 for auto employees, an MOA is not needed at this time. According to OSHA, the agencies will maintain established points of contact, keep lines of communication open, and continue to share information. Furthermore, OSHA officials said regardless of whether MOAs are developed with all DOT component agencies, OSHA has established points of contact at each component agency and will continue to share information with these agencies.

In our past work, we concluded that collaboration is critical when meaningful results that the federal government seeks to achieve require the coordinated efforts of more than one federal agency. [26] Following key practices for effective collaboration can help agencies address a range of challenges, including policy development, program implementation, oversight and monitoring, information sharing and communication, and organizational capacity for training.[27] For this review, we determined that two of the key practices are directly relevant to OSHA's efforts to collaborate with DOT: (1) defining roles, responsibilities, and authorities; and (2) defining outcomes and monitoring progress toward outcomes. OSHA and DOT officials agree that these key practices are beneficial for effective collaboration and believe the key practices we identified have been incorporated in the existing MOAs. However, based on our review of the existing MOAs, we found that the practices were not fully incorporated as discussed below.

Roles and Responsibilities

As our prior work has shown, when agencies work together to define and agree on their respective roles and responsibilities, as well as steps for decision making, clear purposes and goals can be achieved. For example, as part of this effort, agencies can begin to clarify who will do what, identify how to organize their joint and individual efforts, and articulate steps for decision making.[28] Our review of the MOAs between OSHA and DOT components found the agreements document some roles and responsibilities across broad areas of collaboration and provide the framework for working together and defining collaboration, for example:

- Officials from both OSHA and DOT have said that it is in their interests to share information—that is, to identify or refer potential claims of retaliation and safety violations to the other agency. Specifically, if an employee reports a potential safety violation directly to OSHA, it is beneficial for OSHA to refer the employee to DOT since DOT components investigate the allegations of potentially unsafe conditions. To facilitate referrals between the agencies, OSHA's MOAs with FAA [29] and FRA state that when an individual notifies FAA or FRA of alleged discrimination that involves air-carrier or rail-carrier safety, the DOT agencies will inform the individual that a personal remedy is available only through OSHA and that the individual should personally contact OSHA.[30] Additionally, according to OSHA's Whistleblower Investigation Manual, OSHA should provide all incoming retaliation complaints, findings, and orders to the relevant DOT agency.
- OSHA's MOAs with FAA and FRA require OSHA to provide FAA and FRA copies of all complaints and any findings filed under the relevant statute. FAA recently established a secure electronic mailbox designed to receive such complaints and findings from OSHA. Additionally, FAA is using that e-mail mailbox to securely communicate with OSHA to confirm receipt of a complaint or finding, refer a new complaint, and notify staff of safety enforcement actions and outcomes FAA initiated based on OSHA-referred complaints or findings. FRA officials said that all OSHA complaints relevant to FRA are sent to FRA headquarters where they are scanned into a database and reviewed for any potential violations of FRA safety regulations. FRA staff summarizes how FRA handles the complaint and this information is added to FRA's file.

OSHA's current MOAs include general descriptions of the agencies' respective authorities and responsibilities and, according to agency officials, are intended to be broad, flexible agreements to facilitate cooperation. However, the existing MOAs do not clearly define roles with respect to training and regional coordination between the agencies. For example, although the FRA MOA includes information on developing training, the MOA with FAA does not because in general, OSHA officials said a more specific MOA may quickly become outdated or inoperable. Nevertheless, it is unclear which agency—FAA or OSHA—would develop or provide any training to assist FAA enforcement staff in recognizing alleged discrimination complaints that must be referred to OSHA and to assist OSHA staff in recognizing potential violations of federal air safety regulations that should be reported to DOT. OSHA officials said their investigative staff would benefit from additional training because a key challenge the staff face is to fully understand the differences in the transportation industries and statutes. Having roles and responsibilities with respect to training clearly articulated in the FAA MOA (and other MOAs as they are developed) could help ensure such training takes place.

Regarding regional coordination, neither of the existing MOAs specifically defined roles with respect to regional coordination, and as a result, it is not clear or transparent how referrals are coordinated between OSHA and DOT's regional offices. For example, in the case of FRA, before April 2011, each regional office had its own practices for responding to OSHA investigators' requests for whistleblower-related information, which resulted in FRA investigators being unaware of their roles and responsibilities regarding the type of information they could share with OSHA. In April 2011, FRA issued detailed guidance about responding to OSHA's requests for information. FRA developed a centralized approach to respond to OSHA's requests. However, FRA's guidance was issued to FRA's regional offices, and not to OSHA's regional offices and it was unclear whether OSHA's regional investigators were aware of FRA's policies. By more clearly defining agency roles and responsibilities regarding how regional coordination will occur, the agencies may be better able to avoid miscommunication and address inconsistent whistleblower processes involving referrals between the agencies' regional offices.

Outcomes and Monitoring Progress

In September 2012, we concluded that federal agencies engaged in collaborative efforts need to create the means to monitor and evaluate their efforts.[31] Reporting on these activities can help key decision makers within the agencies, as well as clients and stakeholders, to obtain feedback for improving both policy and operational effectiveness. With respect to whistleblower complaints, it would be beneficial for OSHA and DOT to track, monitor, and document the outcomes of the referral processes they have established—that is, the referrals from DOT to OSHA of potential claims of retaliation and the referrals from OSHA to DOT of potential safety violations.[32] Although OSHA's MOAs with FAA and FRA establish these referral processes, the agencies did not develop or document an approach for tracking, monitoring, and overseeing the referral processes. Without such data or developing and documenting an approach, neither OSHA nor DOT can assess whether the referral process is working as intended. OSHA officials said FAA and OSHA are developing a new MOA to streamline the agencies' whistleblower processes for referrals to make them more efficient and consistent. However, since some referrals could involve serious safety concerns from other transportation industries that do not yet have established MOAs with OSHA, it is important that all transportation-related referrals be tracked, monitored, and evaluated. According to OSHA officials, OSHA identifies its intended outcomes for the whistleblower program overall within its operating plan, and specific information on monitoring outcomes of OSHA's collaboration with DOT regarding whistleblower referrals is not included in the plan. We believe by establishing a means to monitor and evaluate the referral processes in the MOAs, OSHA and the DOT component agencies would be able to identify areas for improvement and better ensure that appropriate steps are taken with respect to referrals that include safety violations.

Transportation-Related Whistleblower Claims Have Increased, and Stakeholders Identified Various Factors Potentially Affecting the Number of Claims

Whistleblower Claims Have Increased in the Last 6 Fiscal Years

Overall, the number of transportation-related whistleblower claims increased during the last 6 fiscal years—from 508 in fiscal year 2008 to 821 in fiscal year 2013 (see fig. 3). A sharp rise in claims filed by rail employees, discussed later in this report, accounted for most of the increase in the number of claims. Claims from other transportation industry employees fluctuated during that time. In fiscal year 2013, one whistleblower claim was filed in the auto industry (under the new provisions in MAP-21).

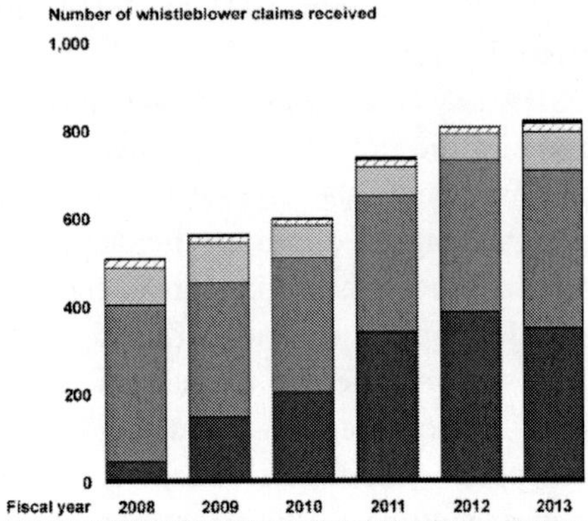

Fiscal year	2008	2009	2010	2011	2012	2013
Moving Ahead for Progress in the 21st Century Act (MAP-21)	N/A	N/A	N/A	N/A	N/A	1
Pipeline Safety Improvement Act (PSIA)	3	3	2	6	2	7
National Transit Systems Security Act (NTSSA)	18	15	14	17	14	19
Wendell H. Ford Aviation Investment and Reform Act for the 21st Century (AIR21)	85	92	75	65	59	86
Surface Transportation Assistance Act (STAA)	357	306	306	312	347	360
Federal Railroad Safety Act (FRSA)	45	145	201	338	384	348
Total	**508**	**561**	**598**	**738**	**806**	**821**

Source: OSHA's whistleblower Protection Porgram statistics.

Figure 3. Number of Whistleblower Claims for Transportation-Related Statutes, Fiscal Years 2008-2013.

Auto industry stakeholders we contacted, including employers and employee representatives, expect the number of whistleblower claims from auto employees to be low because they believe the industry has multiple reporting mechanisms in place, which enables employees to raise safety concerns through those avenues. For example, representatives from the five major auto makers we spoke with noted that a safety-reporting system exists internally within each company, and the companies expect and encourage their employees to report any safety concerns without retaliation. All of the auto makers we contacted said they have a reporting program, such as a hotline, to allow employees to raise safety issues anonymously via the phone or by e-mail, and a process for evaluating and addressing, as appropriate, the reported safety issues. One auto maker we contacted said it has an employee award program, which honors its employees for identifying and reporting any safety concerns on its automobiles, rather than retaliating against employees for raising safety issues. Union officials we contacted also mentioned that grievance procedures and a neutral arbitration process exist internally within one auto company and, as a result, they expect very few whistleblower claims from auto employees at that company. On the other hand, union officials also told us that many auto employees may not be aware of their whistleblower protections under MAP-21, which could also lead to fewer claims with OSHA.

Stakeholders Cited Various Factors That Might Affect the Number of Whistleblower Claims

Stakeholders we contacted consistently identified multiple factors that need to be considered when looking at the number of whistleblower claims filed.[33] These factors are not mutually exclusive and could either increase or decrease the number of whistleblower claims filed with OSHA. The factors include (1) industry-specific characteristics, (2) multiple avenues to address safety issues or a strong safety culture, (3) awareness of whistleblower protection rights, (4) fear of retaliation, (5) statutory whistleblower provisions, and (6) a high number of dismissed claims.

Industry-Specific Characteristics

Stakeholders we contacted consistently cited unique characteristics and cultural differences in each transportation industry as a factor in the number of whistleblower claims. For example, they noted that the number of workers in an industry could play a role. Specifically, a commercial motor vehicle industry official noted that the large number of active truck drivers, compared to the number of employees in other transportation industries contributes to the number of whistleblower claims made by truck drivers. In other words, since there are so many truck drivers, the number of workers who may file a claim might be statistically larger than in other transportation industries. The Bureau of Labor Statistics reported more than 2.2 million employees in the commercial motor vehicle industry, compared to about 1.1 million and 287,000 in the aviation and rail industries, respectively, in 2012.

The presence of labor unions may also contribute to the number of whistleblower claims, according to rail and aviation industry stakeholders we contacted. In a 2011 study of employees and whistleblowers in the work place, the Ethics Resources Center found that union employees, who are often provided certain contractual protections, had much higher rates of reporting specific misconduct than nonunion employees.[34] Officials from OSHA and rail employee groups we contacted also noted that the relationship between employees and management in the rail industry and the working conditions for rail employees has been challenging, such as working up to 16 hours a day and suffering from chronic injuries on the job, which has likely contributed to employees filing more whistleblower claims.

Multiple Avenues to Address Safety Issues or a Strong Safety Culture

The extent to which employees are able to successfully report safety violations also affects the number of potential claims, according to officials from the aviation, pipeline, and public transit industries and unions we interviewed. The availability of multiple safety-reporting mechanisms, such as safety hotlines provided by companies and the industry, can affect whether employees file whistleblower claims. Officials told us that when employees can report safety issues anonymously, they are less fearful of retaliation. Federal safety programs are also available to serve as an avenue for reporting safety issues. For instance, FAA established various voluntary disclosure reporting and partnership programs, which allow aviation employees to report safety concerns and events with protection from legal or disciplinary action by FAA or others, even if the reporting employee caused the safety violation. 35 According to aviation union officials we contacted, this type of collaborative program with labor, management, and FAA may have contributed to the decreasing volume of whistleblower claims since fiscal year 2009, although the numbers have increased in fiscal year 2013. Aviation union officials also noted how such programs have changed the aviation industry culture and allowed employees to report their mistakes and work on resolving safety issues, rather than fearing disciplinary actions or retaliation. Similar to the aviation industry, pipeline union officials we contacted told us that pipeline companies are encouraged to establish an environment where employees can report safety concerns without retaliation. A 2011 survey of employees in the workplace found that employees are more likely to report unlawful or prohibited practices if employees feel confident about their job security and are not worried about retaliation.[36]

Awareness of Whistleblower Protection Rights

Rail-industry and commercial motor-vehicle industry officials we contacted consistently noted employees' awareness of whistleblower protection rights as another factor that may increase or decrease the number of claims. Union officials noted that educating rail employees on whistleblower protection rights may contribute to the higher number of whistleblower claims from rail workers because employees are more aware of their rights. According to rail union officials, they made a concerted effort to educate their members on whistleblower protection rights soon after the Federal Rail Safety

Act was amended in 2007. [37] FRA officials also noted that more rail workers are learning from various sources about OSHA's enforcement of whistleblower protections for rail employees, which might have led to the increase in whistleblower claims.[38] In contrast, pipeline union officials noted that the lower number of whistleblower claims in the pipeline industry may also be attributed to pipeline workers' lack of awareness of OSHA's whistleblower protection program. A union official representing one segment of truck drivers and a whistleblower attorney representing truck drivers cited lack of education on whistleblower protection rights by both employers and employees as a contributing factor to the number of whistleblower claims. On the other hand, this official also noted that long-haul truck drivers and independent owner-operators of trucks may be more aware of whistleblower protection rights than truck drivers in other industries, an awareness that could help explain the high number of whistleblower claims in the commercial motor- vehicle industry.

Fear of Retaliation

Officials representing rail and truck drivers and a whistleblower attorney we contacted said that fear of retaliation is a factor that could cause employees to underreport safety violations and also file fewer whistleblower complaints. For example, officials representing truck drivers noted that truck drivers may break federal safety regulations, such as driving beyond the maximum number of service hours, to avoid getting fired or facing other retaliation from their employers.[39] Independent truck drivers are paid by the mile and are under pressure by employers to extend driving beyond the regulated service hours each day, which may compromise the ability of the drivers to drive trucks safely. Officials representing truck drivers told us that if truck drivers do not want to drive beyond the required service hours and compromise safety, then employers may retaliate in many different ways, including providing no loads (i.e., goods or products) to be delivered. Those representatives and two whistleblower attorneys we contacted said employers can also retaliate by filing fictitious reports on truck drivers, such as reporting that a truck driver abandoned a load, in their employment history, so no one else would hire them.[40] Since truck drivers are afraid of getting "blacklisted" if they make any safety complaints, they may be less likely to report any safety violations. Officials representing independent truck drivers also noted that whistleblower claims may be from new drivers because more experienced drivers are too fearful to file claims. New drivers may also be more aware of whistleblower protections since the Federal Motor Carrier Safety Administration began requiring whistleblower training as part of the entry-level requirements for commercial drivers in July 2004.[41]

Statutory Whistleblower Provisions

Example of a Whistleblower Claim

A truck driver filed a whistleblower claim alleging that his employer violated his rights under the Surface Transportation Assistance Act when the employer blacklisted him and placed an unfavorable notation on his employment report. This retaliation stemmed from the truck driver's refusal to drive an unsafe truck and filing a complaint about violations of commercial vehicle safety regulations related to the unsafe truck. In December 2008, the employee filed a complaint with OSHA. After OSHA investigated the claim, it was appealed through ALJ's and ARB's *de novo* review process. The ARB affirmed ALJ's decision and issued a decision in favor of the employee in June 2012.

Source: GAO Analysis of Administrative Review Board data.

Differences in the statutory provisions related to the number of protected activities and availability of punitive damages may also contribute to variations in the number of filed whistleblower claims, according to rail and public transit officials we contacted. In particular, rail industry officials told us that the larger number of protected activities for rail employees compared with other transportation-related whistleblower statutes has enabled more rail employees to file claims. Rail union officials told us that, on the other hand, the additional protected activities have had a positive effect on rail employees as rail carriers are less likely to retaliate against employees for reporting injuries. The Federal Rail Safety Act provides 12 categories of protected activities for rail employees, including prohibiting employers from retaliating against employees for notifying rail carriers or DOT of a work-related injury or illness and medical and first-aid treatment.[42] Other transportation-related statutes have no such protection for covered employees. According to OSHA officials, about 60 percent of whistleblower claims filed by rail workers involved injury reporting over the years. OSHA recently began meeting with representatives from air, rail, and trucking industries to discuss the effectiveness of existing legislation in addressing practices that threaten employees' ability to raise safety concerns, among other things.[43] Additionally, rail industry officials told us that the availability of punitive damages in some statutes may be another contributing factor to the number of whistleblower claims. Rail, trucking, and pipeline employees are eligible to receive punitive damages if OSHA determines their whistleblower claims to be of merit. Rail industry officials noted that after the Federal Rail Safety Act was amended in 2007, increasing the amount of punitive damages that could be collected, the number of claims from rail workers began increasing.[44]

High Number of Dismissed Claims

Officials representing rail, aviation, and public transit employees and truck drivers, and a whistleblower attorney told us that the high number of dismissed claims may discourage other employees, who may believe they have been retaliated against, from filing a claim. As shown in figure 4, some 49 percent of transportation-related claims OSHA closed in fiscal year 2013 were dismissed, while 3 percent of the claims were found to have merit. According to OSHA officials, whistleblower claims were dismissed for various reasons, including that the claims were filed past the deadline or had insufficient evidence to demonstrate the employer had violated the whistleblower provisions. Additionally, about 52 percent (64) of the 123 claims that were closed by the OALJ and about 66 percent (19) of 29 claims that were closed by ARB in fiscal year 2012 were also dismissed. More information on the disposition of transportation-related whistleblower claims that were closed in fiscal year 2012 by OALJ and ARB can be found in appendix III.[45]

Officials representing rail, aviation, and public transit employees and truck drivers we contacted attributed the high number of dismissed claims to inconsistent investigation and significant differences in the investigation of whistleblower claims among OSHA's regional offices; the officials told us that while the investigative process is fair and reasonable in some regional offices, other regional offices are not. Another official representing transportation employees told us that there could be a different investigation process and decision for the same type of whistleblower claim depending on which OSHA regional office was handling the claim.

Transportation-related statutes	Merit	Settled[a]	Kicked out[b]	Dismissed	Withdrawn	Total number of closed cases
Federal Railroad Safety Act (FRSA)	17 (4%)	110 (28%)	34 (9%)	173 (43%)	65 (16%)	399
Surface Transportation Assistance Act (STAA)	11 (3%)	83 (22%)	5 (1%)	191 (51%)	85 (23%)	375
Wendell H. Ford Aviation Investment and Reform Act (AIR21)	2 (2%)	18 (20%)	N/A	53 (60%)	15 (17%)	88
Pipeline Safety Improvement Act (PSIA)	0	0	N/A	5 (83%)	1 (17%)	6
National Transit Systems Security Act (NTSSA)	0	1 (9%)	0	5 (45%)	5 (45%)	11
Total	30 (3%)	212 (24%)	39 (4%)	427 (49%)	171 (19%)	879

Source: OSHA's Whistleblower Protection Program statistics.

Note: Percentages may not sum to 100 because of rounding.

[a] The number of settled claims includes both settlements where OSHA investigators actively assisted both parties (complainant and respondent) in reaching an agreement, where possible, and those where OSHA did not participate in the settlement negotiations. Settled claims may also have merit, but they were categorized as "settled" if both parties reached an agreement.

[b] Kicked out claims are those filed under FRSA, STAA, and NTSSA, where the complainants decided to file civil actions in federal district courts for de novo review, where there had been no final decision of the Secretary of Labor within 210 days of filing the claim, and there had been no delay due to the complainant's bad faith.

Figure 4. Disposition of Transportation-Related Whistleblower Claims That OSHA Closed in Fiscal Year 2013.

In September 2010, the Department of Labor's Office of Inspector General reported that OSHA did not always ensure that whistleblower claims were appropriately investigated and could not provide assurance that complainants were protected as intended under the various whistleblower protection statutes.46 The DOL-OIG recommended, among other things, that OSHA oversee and monitor investigations, and OSHA agreed. OSHA officials told us that steps have been taken to improve the investigative process, such as further training of investigators and increased staffing. In December 2013, OSHA completed its first regional audit. OSHA is also planning to establish a work group to look at developing a consistent process for OSHA's regions to use when they conduct case file audits of the whistleblower program. OSHA plans to establish the work group in March 2014 and plans to develop a process by September 2014. OSHA plans to incorporate this process into OSHA's overall audit process.

Although the number of transportation-related whistleblower claims has increased in the last 6 years, the reported number of claims can be interpreted various ways, yielding little meaningful information. For example, a low number of whistleblower claims could mean that employees are not retaliated against for reporting safety violations. But a low number of claims could also mean that employees are so fearful of retaliation that they choose not to report safety violations in the first place, or even that employees who have been retaliated against for reporting a safety violation are so discouraged by the high number of dismissed claims that they choose not to file a claim. Our interviews with key stakeholders revealed numerous factors that could affect the number of claims made. Because of the factors identified by stakeholders, it is difficult to use the number of claims as an indication of whether employees are taking appropriate advantage of their protections under whistleblower laws.

CONCLUSION

The ability of transportation workers to report safety violations or other unsafe conditions without fear of reprisal is protected by law. While OSHA has primary responsibility for administering the Whistleblower Protection Program for these workers, collaboration with DOT is critical because of DOT's role to enforce the underlying safety provisions of the transportation-related whistleblower statutes. Consistent with key practices for effective collaboration, OSHA and DOT document their agreements through MOAs that are publicly available, and at the time of our review, the agencies had two existing MOAs and were in the process of developing MOAs for almost all of the other transportation industries. There are opportunities to strengthen these MOAs by following key practices for effective collaboration, especially related to (1) clearly delineating roles and responsibilities for training and regional coordination and (2) monitoring program outcomes. It is unclear which agencies will develop training and how they will coordinate their regional offices' activities and how the referral processes will be monitored to ensure that goals and desired outcomes are achieved. Clearly delineating roles and responsibilities for conducting training and for coordinating regional offices' activities could help ensure that training occurs and that the agencies avoid miscommunication and inconsistent processes involving referrals between their regional offices. Additionally, lacking clarity on how the agencies will evaluate and report on the results of the referral processes, the agencies are unable to identify areas for improvement and ensure that appropriate steps are taken on safety violations. Finally, if OSHA and DOT do not build these practices into their ongoing efforts to develop their MOAs, they may miss an opportunity to enhance and sustain interagency collaboration through these MOAs.

RECOMMENDATION FOR EXECUTIVE ACTION

We recommend that the Secretaries of Labor and Transportation evaluate their current and in-process MOAs to ensure that the MOAs incorporate key practices for collaboration, such as those practices highlighted in this report.

AGENCY COMMENTS AND OUR EVALUATION

We provided a draft of this report to the Departments of Labor and Transportation for their review and comment. The Department of Labor provided written comments, as well as technical comments. The Department of Transportation provided technical comments only. We incorporated the technical comments from both agencies as appropriate.

Neither agency stated whether they agreed or disagreed with the recommendation that the agencies assess their current and in-process MOAs and incorporate key practices for collaboration. While DOT did not address the recommendation, OSHA said that it believed its current and pending MOAs do incorporate the key collaboration practices that we identified in this report but agreed that there was room for improvement in the implementation of these key practices when collaborating with DOT's agencies. We did not assess the extent to which the key practices were actually being implemented. However, as discussed in this report, the existing MOAs do not clearly define roles and responsibilities with respect to training and regional coordination between the agencies, and the agencies did not develop or document an approach for tracking, monitoring, and overseeing the referral process. Thus, we continue to believe that there are opportunities to strengthen the existing MOAs by better delineating roles and responsibilities and monitoring program outcomes that may help inform the implementation of such practices. Moreover, because the pending MOAs were not made available for our review, we were not able to determine whether they contained the key practices.

In technical comments, both agencies also noted that for certain industries with low complaint volume such as auto employees, they are assessing whether MOAs were needed at this time. We believe this approach is contradictory to the agencies' position that MOAs are a key way they document their collaboration.

Additionally, as we found in this report, it is difficult to use the number of claims as an indication of whether employees are taking appropriate advantage of their protections under whistleblower laws, and so it is not clear why the agencies would use this as a determinant in their decision. Finally, for auto employees, considering that this law recently passed and OSHA is still establishing procedures for how it will address such claims, it is not surprising that the number of claims filed to date is low.

As a result, we encourage OSHA and DOT to consider these factors as they assess the need for MOAs.

Lori Rectanus
Acting Director,
Physical Infrastructure Issues

APPENDIX I: DIFFERENCES IN THE TRANSPORTATION-RELATED WHISTLEBLOWER STATUTES

OSHA is responsible for administering the whistleblower protection provisions of six transportation-related federal statutes. These statutes are supplemented by regulations that set forth specific requirements for the whistleblower protection process. Such a process often includes an investigation, an administrative review (which can include the Office of Administrative Law Judges (OALJ) and the Administrative Review Board (ARB), and potential legal action in a U.S. court. Many provisions of the statutes are similar, including a 60-day deadline for determining the initial findings of an OSHA investigation, a *de novo* review of appealed whistleblower claims, and some remedies, such as back pay. There are key differences in the whistleblower protection process, as shown in figure 5.

Transportation-related statutes	Deadline to file complaint		Deadline for appealing to the ALJ		Deadline for the ARB's final decision		If the Secretary has not issued a final decision within 210 days of the complaint, the complainant can bring an action in U.S. District Court	Punitive damages Ordered by the Secretary and enforceable by the Court	Fines for frivolous complaints[a]
	90 days	180 days	30 days	60 days	90 days after the hearing concludes	120 days after the hearing concludes			
Moving Ahead for Progress in the 21st Century Act (MAP-21)		✓	✓			✓	✓		✓
Federal Railroad Safety Act (FRSA)		✓	✓			✓	✓	✓	
Surface Transportation Assistance Act (STAA)		✓	✓			✓	✓	✓	
Wendell H. Ford Aviation Investment and Reform Act (AIR21)	✓		✓			✓			✓
Pipeline Safety Improvement Act (PSIA)		✓		✓	✓				✓
National Transit Systems Security Act (NTSSA)		✓	✓			✓	✓	✓	✓

Acronyms:
Office of Administrative Law Judges (ALJ)
Administrative Review Board (ARB)

Source: GAO analysis of relevant statutes and regulations.

Note: Secretary determines that a complaint is frivolous or brought in bad faith, the Secretary may award the employer a reasonable attorney's fee not exceeding $1,000.

Figure 5. Key Differences in the Whistleblower Protection Process of the Transportation-Related Statutes.

APPENDIX II: OBJECTIVES, SCOPE, AND METHODOLOGY

The Moving Ahead for Progress in the 21st Century (MAP-21) mandated that we review efforts to include auto industry employees in the Occupational Safety and Health Administration's (OSHA) Whistleblower Protection Program and provide information on the differences in the statutory provisions and the disposition of transportation-related whistleblower claims. This report presents information on (1) the steps OSHA has taken to include auto industry employees in its whistleblower program and the extent to which OSHA has collaborated with DOT components to address potential safety violations, and (2) the number of transportation-related whistleblower claims in the last 6 years and stakeholder-identified factors that might affect those numbers.

To address these issues, we examined the whistleblower provisions of the six relevant transportation-related statutes: (1) MAP-21, (2) the Federal Railroad Safety Act, (3) the National Transit Systems Security Act, (4) the Surface Transportation Assistance Act, (5) the Pipeline Safety Improvement

Act, and (6) the Wendell H. Ford Aviation Investment and Reform Act for the 21st Century. These statutes cover transportation industry employees and do not cover federal employees who work in DOT. We also reviewed our previous reports on whistleblower protection. To examine OSHA's efforts to include auto industry employees in whistleblower protection, we reviewed pertinent documentation from OSHA and DOT on whistleblower protection and interviewed key agency officials from OSHA's Whistleblower Protection Program and DOT components on coordinating efforts to administer whistleblower protection for transportation industry employees. To determine the extent to which OSHA and DOT incorporated key practices for effective collaboration, we reviewed regulations authorizing DOT to enter into MOAs with OSHA in regard to setting and enforcing occupational safety or health standards and whistleblower protections,[1] and identified key practices to apply to interagency collaborative efforts based on our past work on leading collaboration practices.[2] We reviewed the key practices[3] and selected two key practices for interagency collaborative efforts—defining roles and responsibilities and outcomes and monitoring progress—because they were the most relevant to our review of OSHA's and DOT's collaborative efforts. We analyzed and compared memorandums of agreements that were available between OSHA and DOT component agencies to determine the extent to which the agencies were following key practices for implementing interagency collaborative mechanisms. In completing our work, we did not assess the effectiveness of OSHA's Whistleblower Protection Program because GAO had recently reviewed the effectiveness of the program.[4]

To assess the number of transportation-related whistleblower claims, we analyzed OSHA data on the number of whistleblower claims received from fiscal years 2008 to 2013 and the disposition of claims that were closed in fiscal year 2013. We selected data starting from fiscal year 2008 to include the number of claims from rail and public transit employees that filed with OSHA in the first year after the enactment of the National Transit Systems Security Act and amendment of the Federal Rail Safety Act in 2007. To determine the reliability of OSHA's data on whistleblower claims, we reviewed our previous reports recommending improvements on OSHA's data on whistleblower complaints and assessed the status of OSHA's implementing our recommendations, including reviewing relevant documentation, and interviewing cognizant officials about their processes for reviewing the data and ensuring their accuracy. In general, based on the corrective actions that were taken, we consider the data used to be sufficiently reliable with attribution to official sources for the purposes of providing information on the number of transportation-related whistleblower complaints received in fiscal years 2008 to 2013 and information on the disposition of transportation-related whistleblower claims that OSHA closed in fiscal year 2013. We focused on the disposition of claims in fiscal year 2013 since the corrective actions were taken over time and earlier disposition data are likely to be less reliable. We also analyzed data on the disposition of transportation-related whistleblower claims that the Office of Administrative Law Judges and Administrative Review Board closed to examine other possible disposition of claims in the whistleblower review process. We used data from fiscal year 2012 from these two agencies because it was the most recent data available to us during the time of our review. We used the Bureau of Labor Statistics Current Employment Survey to obtain data on the 2012 average annual number of employees in the different transportation sectors.

To identify factors affecting the number of whistleblower claims, we reviewed literature on whistleblower protection and interviewed stakeholders in the different transportation industries, including officials from 44 organizations representing employees and employers and nonprofit and advocacy groups representing whistleblowers to obtain their perspective on factors that impact the filing of whistleblower claims. Table 1 below provides a list of all the stakeholders we interviewed, including government officials and industry representatives in the different transportation industries. We selected these stakeholders because among other things, we had previously identified them as significant stakeholders in the transportation industries, and they represented a significant number of members in each of the six transportation industries; they were also referred by other stakeholders, including federal government officials and experts in whistleblower issues.

Table 1. Government Officials and Industry Representatives We Interviewed

Stakeholder groups	Stakeholder
Federal government agency officials	Department of Labor: •Occupational Safety and Health Administration •Office of Administrative Law Judges •Administrative Review Board •Office of Inspector General Department of Transportation:

Stakeholder groups	Stakeholder
	•Federal Aviation Administration •Federal Motor Carrier Safety Administration •Federal Railroad Administration •Federal Transit Administration •National Highway Traffic Safety Administration •Pipeline and Hazardous Materials Safety Administration •Office of Inspector General
Organizations Representing Employees	•Government Accountability Project •National Whistleblower Center •AFL-CIO, Transportation Trade Department •Commercial Vehicle Safety Alliance •Truckers Justice Center Automobiles: •International Association of Machinist, Auto Mechanics Local 701 •United Auto Workers Aviation: •Airline Pilots Association •American Federation of Flight Attendants •International Brotherhood of Teamsters, Airline Division Motor Carriers: •International Brotherhood of Teamsters •Owner-Operator Independent Driver Association Pipeline: •International Brotherhood of Electrical Workers •International Brotherhood of Teamsters,

Table 1. (Continued)

Stakeholder groups	Stakeholder
	Pipeline Division •International Union of Operating Engineers •United Association, Pipeliners Local 798 Public Transit: •American Federation of State, County and Municipal Employees •Transport Workers Union •Union Transportation Union Rail: •American Train Dispatchers Association •Brotherhood of Locomotive Engineers and Trainmen •Brotherhood of Maintenance of Ways Employees Division •Transportation Communications International Union
Organizations Representing Industry Employers	Automobile: •Ford •General Motors •Honda •National Automobile Dealers Association •Nissan •Toyota Aviation: •Airlines for America •National Air Transportation Association •Regional Airline Association Motor Carriers: •American Bus Association •American Trucking Association

Stakeholder groups	Stakeholder
	Pipeline: •American Gas Association •American Petroleum Institute •American Pipeline Contractors Association •Association of Oil Pipe Lines •Common Ground Alliance Public Transit: •American Public Transportation Association •Community Transportation Association Rail: •American Short Line and Regional Railroad Association •Association of American Railroads •National Railroad Construction and Maintenance Association

Source: GAO.

Based on our interviews with stakeholders, we identified and synthesized the factors under major themes. One aspect of the analysis was to discern the extent to which a factor was common to all transportation sectors or associated with a few or just one sector. The factors we report are limited to those identified by the stakeholders noted above and may not include all factors that could be identified. Also, the factors that we have identified should not be viewed as being representative of all transportation sector representatives and stakeholders. However, the factors identified are illustrative of key issues affecting the number of whistleblower claims that were consistently raised by the various stakeholders.

We conducted this performance audit from May 2013 to March 2014 in accordance with generally accepted government auditing standards. Those standards require that we plan and perform the audit to obtain sufficient, appropriate evidence to provide a reasonable basis for our findings and conclusions based on our audit objectives. We believe that the evidence obtained provides a reasonable basis for our findings and conclusions based on our audit objectives.

APPENDIX III: DISPOSITION OF WHISTLEBLOWER CLAIMS FROM THE OFFICE OF ADMINISTRATIVE LAW JUDGES AND ADMINISTRATIVE REVIEW BOARD

After OSHA investigates a whistleblower claim and makes a finding, either party to the claim may appeal OSHA's finding to the Office of Administrative Law Judges. After the Office of Administrative Law Judges reviews and issues a decision, the finding can further be appealed to the Administrative Review Board. Most of the claims that the Office of Administrative Law Judges and Administrative Review Board decided in fiscal year 2012 have been dismissed or withdrawn.[1] Some reasons for dismissal included: employee failure to meet one or more elements of a claim, lack of timeliness of complaint, or employee abandonment of the claim. Figures 6 and 7 illustrate the disposition of whistleblower claims that were closed in fiscal year 2012 from the Office of Administrative Law Judges and the Administrative Review Board, respectively.

Transportation-related statutes	Favorable to complainant	Settled	Dismissed	Withdrawn	Total
Federal Railroad Safety Act (FRSA)	3 (7%)	13 (30%)	22 (51%)	5 (12%)	43
Surface Transportation Assistance Act (STAA)	4 (7%)	18 (32%)	28 (49%)	7 (12%)	57
Wendell H. Ford Aviation Investment and Reform Act (AIR21)	2 (12%)	3 (18%)	10 (59%)	2 (12%)	17
Pipeline Safety Improvement Act (PSIA)	0	0	1 (100%)	0	1
National Transit Systems Security Act (NTSSA)	2 (40%)	0	3 (60%)	0	5
Total	11 (9%)	34 (28%)	64 (52%)	14 (11%)	123

Source: GAO analysis of the Office of Administrative Law Judges data.

Note: Percentages may not sum to 100 because of rounding.

[a]Settled claims may also have merit but they were categorized as "settled" if both parties reached an agreement.

Figure 6. Disposition of Whistleblower Claims That the Office of Administrative Law Judges Closed in Fiscal Year 2012.

Transportation-related statutes	Favorable to complainant[a]		Dismissed[b]		Settled[c]	Withdrawn by either party	Denied review
	Merit	Procedural	Merit	Procedural			
Federal Railroad Safety Act (FRSA)	0	0	1	2	0	0	0
Surface Transportation Assistance Act (STAA)	1	3	5	4	0	1	2
Wendell H. Ford Aviation Investment and Reform Act (AIR21)	1	0	4	2	0	0	0
Pipeline Safety Improvement Act (PSIA)	0	0	0	0	0	0	0
National Transit Systems Security Act (NTSSA)	0	1	0	1	1	0	0
Total	2	4	10	9	1	1	2

Source: GAO analysis of Administrative Review Board Data.

Note: Whistleblower claims that reversed the Office of Administrative Law Judges' (OALJ) decisions and/or remanded it back to OALJ were not included in this analysis. Claims that did not fall under the categories above were also excluded.

[a] Of the 29 whistleblower claims that the Administrative Review Board closed in fiscal year 2012, 6 (or about 21 percent) were found favorable to complainants based on merit or procedural grounds.

[b] Of the 29 whistleblower claims that the Administrative Review Board closed in fiscal year 2012, 19 (or about 66 percent) were dismissed based on merit or procedural grounds.

[c] Settled claims may also have merit, but they were categorized as "settled' if both parties reached an agreement an agreement.

Figure 7. Disposition of Whistleblower Claims That the Administrative Review Board Closed in Fiscal Year 2012.

End Notes

[1] The transportation industries are automotive, aviation, commercial motor carriers, pipeline, public transit, and rail.

[2] In all, OSHA is responsible for investigating whistleblower claims under 22 statutes.

[3] Pub. L. No. 112-141, § 31307, 126 Stat. 405, 765 (2012).

[4] Pub. L. No. 112-141, § 31307(b), 126 Stat. 405, 765 (2012).

[5] These statutes cover transportation industry employees, not federal government employees who work for DOT.

[6] 49 U.S.C. § 30171.

[7] 49 U.S.C. § 20109.

[8] 6 U.S.C. § 1142.

[9] 49 U.S.C. § 31105.

[10] 49 U.S.C. § 60129.

[11] 49 U.S.C. § 42121.

[12] GAO, Managing for Results: Key Considerations for Implementing Interagency Collaborative Mechanisms, GAO-12-1022, (Washington, D.C.: Sept. 27, 2012). In conducting its work, GAO interviewed experts in the field of collaboration, reviewed collaborative mechanisms used by federal agencies, and reviewed and analyzed literature on interagency collaborative mechanisms.

[13] GAO, Whistleblower Protection Program: Better Data and Improved Oversight Would Help Ensure Program Quality and Consistency, GAO-09-106, (Washington, D.C.: Jan. 27, 2009).

[14] 29 C.F.R. §§ 1978, 1979, 1981, 1982, and 1983.

[15] GAO-09-106.

[16] Additional information about the status of these recommendations is available at http://www.gao.gov/products/GAO-09-106.

[17] During our review, OSHA initially planned to develop a memorandum of agreement (MOA) with the National Highway Traffic Safety Administration (NHTSA) for auto employees covered under MAP-21. In their technical comments on a draft of this report, the agencies said OSHA and NHTSA agreed that due to the low complaint volume under MAP-21, an MOA was not needed at this time.

[18] When an agency finds that it has good cause to issue a final rule without first publishing a proposed rule, it often characterizes the rule as an “interim final rule,” or “interim rule.” This type of rule typically becomes effective immediately upon publication. In most cases, the agency stipulates that it will alter the interim rule if warranted by public comments. If the agency decides not to make changes to the interim rule, it generally will publish a brief final rule in the Federal Register confirming that decision. We did not review the interim final rule because it was being developed during our review.

[19] The regulatory agenda is how agencies announce future rulemaking activities and update the public on pending and completed regulatory activities.

[20] OSHA’s Whistleblower Investigations Manual provides guidance for investigating complaints of retaliation under all the whistleblower statutes administered by OSHA.

[21] Pub. L. No. 110-314, § 219, 122 Stat. 3016, 3062 (2008).

[22] OSHA has developed and posted fact sheets for other transportation industry employees in aviation, commercial motor carriers, pipeline, public transportation agencies, and railroad workers.

[23] Since 1993, DOT’s component agencies have been authorized to enter into MOAs with OSHA in regard to setting and enforcing occupational safety or health standards and whistleblower protections for employees in DOT-regulated industries. 49 C.F.R.§ 1.81(a)(23).

[24] In OSHA’s technical comments, OSHA said the agency is considering whether certain MOAs are necessary, specifically those involving transportation statutes with low complaint volume.

[25] We were unable to review any draft of MOAs because they were in the beginning stages of development during our review.

[26] GAO-12-1022.

[27] GAO-12-1022. The key practices for collaboration include outcomes and accountability, bridging organizational cultures, leadership, clarity of roles and responsibilities, participants, resources, and written guidance and agreements.

[28] GAO-12-1022.

[29] Although FAA refers to its agreement as a memorandum of understanding, in this report we use MOAs to refer to agreements between OSHA and DOT components.

30 There is no direct referral from DOT to OSHA. It is left to the individual employee whether he or she wants to file a claim with OSHA.

[31] GAO-12-1022.

[32] When employees contact DOT about a potential claim of retaliation, DOT informs the employees that they should contact OSHA directly to file a claim.

[33] The factors were commonly identified by stakeholders; however, not all stakeholders identified each factor.

[34] Ethics Resource Center, Inside the Mind of a Whistleblower: A Supplemental Report of the 2011 National Business Ethics Survey, Arlington, VA (2012).

[35] The goal of FAA's Aviation Safety Action Program is to enhance aviation safety through the prevention of accidents and incidents. Its focus is to encourage voluntary reporting of safety issues and events that come to the attention of employees of certain aircraft certificate holders (i.e., aircraft carriers). The program is based on a safety partnership that includes the FAA and air carriers as well as any third party entities, such as the employee's labor organization. Other self-reported safety programs include the Voluntary Disclosure Reporting Program. For more information on these safety programs, see GAO, Aviation Safety: Enhanced Oversight and Improved Availability of Risk-Based Data Control Could Further Improve Safety, GAO-12-24 (Washington, DC: Oct. 5, 2011) and GAO, Aviation Safety: Improved Data Quality and Analysis Capabilities Are Needed as FAA Plans a Risk-Based Approach to Safety Oversight, GAO-10-414 (Washington, DC: May 6, 2012).

[36] Ethics Resource Center, Inside the Mind of a Whistleblower: A Supplemental Report of the 2011 National Business Ethics Survey, Arlington, VA (2012).

[37] The Federal Rail Safety Act was amended by the Implementing Recommendations of the 9/11 Commission Act of 2007, Pub.L.No. 110-53, 121 Stat. 444.

[38] FRA officials also told us that FRA's witness statement form, which is used for enforcement activities, includes information about whistleblower protections and where to file a claim with OSHA.

[39] Most drivers are subject to the Hours of Service regulations, if they drive commercial motor vehicles. The Hours of Service regulations differs for property-carrying drivers and passenger-carrying drivers (e.g., Greyhound bus drivers). Passenger-carrying drivers may not drive after having been on duty for 15 hours, following 8 consecutive hours off duty, while property-carrying drivers may not drive beyond the 14th consecutive hour after coming on duty, following 10 consecutive hours off duty. (49 C.F.R. Part 395).

[40] As part of a pre-hiring procedure, nearly all large trucking companies will look at a trucker's employment and driving record to see if there is any history of accidents, traffic violations, or other issues that might disqualify the driver from the job. HireRight collects all this information into its database and sells the information on individual drivers as a Drive-a-Check report.

[41] All entry-level drivers who drive in interstate commerce and are subject to the commercial drivers license requirements of 49 C.F.R. Part 383 must comply with the rules of Entry-Level Driver Training Requirements of 49 C.F.R. Part 380, Subpart E. Drivers who are subject to the jurisdiction of the Federal Transit Administration or who are otherwise exempt under 49 C.F.R. § 390.3(f) are exempt. Information on whistleblower protections is included as part of the Entry-Level Driver Training Requirements. See 69 Fed. Reg. 29384 (May 21, 2004).

[42] 49 U.S.C. § 20109.

[43] The meeting with representatives from air, rail, and trucking industries is part of the Whistleblower Protection Advisory Committee's Transportation Sector Working Group that was charged to consider the effects and successes of the existing laws, gaps in both legislation and employer practices, employer practices that raise particular concerns, and the effectiveness of current legislation and enforcement in addressing these gaps. According to

OSHA officials, the purpose of the working group is to obtain advice on where and how to most effectively and productively focus OSHA's enforcement and outreach to the industries to achieve the greatest impact, given its current resources.

[44] The Federal Rail Safety Act was amended by the Implementing Recommendations of the 9/11 Commission Act of 2007, Pub.L.No. 110-53, 121 Stat 444.

[45] We used data from fiscal year 2012 from these two agencies because it was the most recent data available to us during the time of our review.

[46] Department of Labor Office of Inspector General, Complainant Did Not Always Receive Appropriate Investigation Under the Whistleblower Protection Program, Report Number 02-10-202-10-105 (Washington, D.C.: Sept. 30, 2010).

End Notes for Appendix II

[1] 49 C.F.R. § 1.81 (a)(23).

[2] GAO, Managing for Results: Key Considerations for Implementing Interagency Collaborative Mechanisms, GAO-12-1022, (Washington, D.C.: Sept. 27, 2012).

[3] GAO-12-1022. The key practices for collaboration include outcomes and accountability, bridging organizational cultures, leadership, clarity of roles and responsibilities, participants, resources, and written guidance and agreements.

[4] GAO-09-106.

End Note for Appendix III

[1] We used fiscal year 2012 data from the two agencies because it was the most recent data available during the time of our review.

INDEX

D

E

F